# Hobbyist Guide

## —— To ——

# The Natural Aquarium

AQUARIUM DIGEST INTERNATIONAL
—— COLLECTOR'S EDITION ——

# Hobbyist Guide
## —— To ——
# The Natural Aquarium

Dr. Chris Andrews

© 1991
**Tetra-Press**
TetraWerke Dr. rer nat. Ulrich Baensch GmbH
P.O.Box 1580, D-4520 Melle, Germany
All rights reserved, incl. film, broadcasting, television as well as the reprinting
1st edition 1–10.000, 1991
Printed in Germany
Distributed in U.S.A. by
Tetra Sales (Division of Warner-Lambert)
Morris Plains, N.J. 07950
Distributed in UK by Tetra Sales, Lambert Court,
Chestnut Avenue, Eastleigh Hampshire 505 3ZQ
WL-Code: 16581

**ISBN 3-89356-132-3**

# CONTENTS

# Editorial Comments

Dr. Chris Andrews

In this special combined re-issue of the *Aquarium Digest International* we deal with aquarium plants and, in particular, the creation of beautiful underwater aquascapes.

Most fishkeepers would, of course, like to have a beautifully planted aquarium, but experience difficulties in growing plants successfully. Based on information provided by a number of european aquarists and leading aquarium plant experts, the concept of the "natural aquarium" is introduced where fish and plants live in harmony in a very naturalistic setting. The environmental requirements of plants are emphasised especially with regard to lighting, pH, water hardness, the tank base medium, and so on. Some plants even require additional fertilisers from time to time.

Most good aquatic stores can provide an excellent choice of plants, fish decorative materials and equipment, that will enable you to create specific underwater habitats. Such a tank might contain fish and plants from a certain geographic area, or simply particular kinds of fish and plants which share similar environmental preferences. But do not let yourself by limited by what you read in books – be prepared to experiment. After all, that is what fishkeeping is all about.

Further information can be found in other issues of the ADI or in the books in the *Tetra* series, particularly "A Fishkeepers Guide to Aquarium Plants" by Barry James.

*Dr. Chris Andrews*

*Sri Lanka, origin of many popular aquatic plants.*

*An example of a fully planted natural aquarium . . . waiting for fish to be selected.*

# PLANTS AND FISH

One objective of every enthusiastic tropical fish hobbyist should be to replicate the natural environment in a home aquarium. A natural environment for most tropical fish includes live plants. This "natural aquarium" is also referred to as a "balanced" aquarium since fish and plants complement each other. This occurs in two important ways. First, natural plants consume the nitrogenous waste products produced by

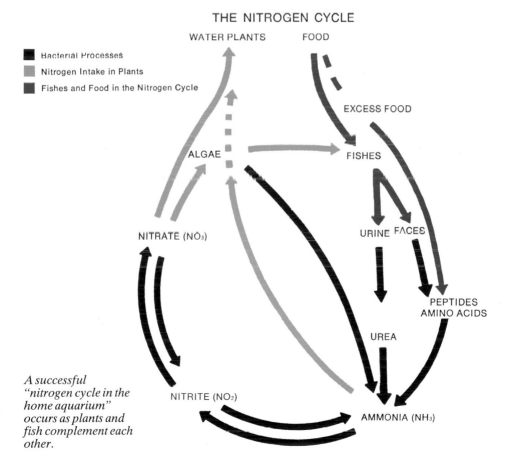

THE NITROGEN CYCLE

A successful "nitrogen cycle in the home aquarium" occurs as plants and fish complement each other.

by fish and convert these waste products into nutrients for their growth. This prevents a build-up of nitrogen toxicity in the aquarium and helps maintain what is commonly called the nitrogen cycle. Secondly, fish require oxygen which plants release, and plants require carbon dioxide which fish release. This forms the basis for the process of photosynthesis. In a successfully functioning natural aquarium, plants and fish help or complement one another. This is not only beautiful to look at but it gives the hobbyist a true sense of accomplishment.

By reading through this issue of the ADI, you will learn how to select the essential life-support equipment for a natural aquarium, how to care for your fish and plants, and how to simulate specific natural habitats such as an Amazon basin or a quiet stream in Southeast Asia, you will truly appreciate the joy of a home aquarium. One word of advice. Wherever possible, select good quality products. This is true whether you have a natural aquarium or one utilizing artifical plants. But for a natural aquarium it is particularly true in such areas as heating and lighting which are so essential to the success of live plants. Full-spectrum or equivalent fluorescent lightning is significantly more expensive than ordinary bulbs. To the naked eye their difference might not be significant, but for aquarium plants the differences are very significant. The old adage "you get what you pay for" is very true in selecting products for a home aquarium.

*Ramirez's dwarf cichlid is beautiful but a little delicate (see page 125)*
*Photo: H. Linke*

▷
*A "natural aquarium"*
*adds a new dimension*
*to aqaurium enjoyment*
*and challenge.*

# PLANTS AND THE AQUARIUM

As we are all aware, aquariums come in a variety of sizes. Most beginning hobbyists start with a 38 litre or 76 litre (10 or 20 gallon) tank and as they become more advanced they soon add or „trade-up" to larger sizes. You will learn after you have read the various sections on available aquarium plants that many plants require aquariums that are 45–60 cm (18 to 24 inches) in depth. This depth allows most plants to grow to their full size and also allows these larger plants, and in particular those requiring full light, to be kept with smaller plants which require partial shade. By proper planting, the leaves of the larger plants will provide shade for the smaller, shade-requiring plants. The hobbyist interested in the truly successful all natural aquarium should select the biggest aquarium practical a 114 l (30 gallons) tank would be a starter size for a natural aquarium, and aquariums over 380 l (100 gallons) make breathtaking environments through terracing and more varieties of fish.

In selecting your natural aquarium and its location, some important criteria should be recognized. First, the aquarium should be placed out of direct sunlight. Although

plants require simulated sunlight, it is much more advantageous in controlling their growth and in minimizing algae to utilize special flourescent fixtures rather than natural sunlight. Secondly, a natural aquarium requires maintenance and that includes regular water changes, it is therefore desirable to place the aquarium near to a water supply and to recognize that if it is to be placed on expensive carpeting or flooring, precautions must be taken against spilling. Yet another important factor is a stand. Under the subject of filtration you will quickly learn that a natural aquarium utilizing an undergravel filter is not desirable unless each plant is individually potted. This is not always desired since most plants must have room to progagate by producing "runners" and this is not possible when potted. Therefore an outside power filter or a foam filter are preferable. Since some power filters must be positioned outside, and below the aquarium water level, it is recommended that the aquarium be placed on a firm stand designed as a cabinet or console. While most tropical fish stores have these stands available, they are simply and decoratively constructed utilizing strong wood and decorative panelling.

Another important factor in selecting the aquarium is recognizing that plants require specialized fluorescent lighting. These special tubes must provide full-spectrum lighting, i.e. that lighting which best duplicates natural sunlight. Therefore, depending on the size of the aquarium, a reflector hood or a glass canopy cover with reflector strips must be included with the complete unit.

## Lighting for the natural aquarium

The major difference between an aquarium utilizing artifical plants and one in which natural plants are to be kept is the importance of the lighting requirements. In an artificially planted aquarium you can utilize incandescent bulbs or a variety of fluorescent tubes.

A major advantage of a natural aquarium is the life-support process by which plants and fish complement each other. This is called photosynthesis. During periods of light, fish consume oxygen and release carbon dioxide, while plants consume carbon dioxide and in turn release oxygen. This important complementary process benefits the health of both fish and plants and creates a "balanced aquarium". Additionally, the plants consume the nitrogenous waste the fish. This contributes to a successful nitrogen cycle which is so important to the on-going health and well-being of the fish. A balanced or natural aquarium requires proper "full-spectrum" or equivalent lighting and also requires that tubes are changed regularly.

Full-spectrum light is explained as that light which simulates sunlight in a home aquarium. *Only* through the use of full-spectrum light can aquatic plants prosper. Your dealer can recommend a full-spectrum tube or a tube having equivalent results on plant growth. These tubes generally claim to have a life expectancy of 20000 hours; however, you should realistically expect less than one-half of this to be

*Photosynthesis only occurs in bright light, and not at all at night.*

suitable for a natural aquarium. This will vary somewhat depending on the lighting demands of your selected plants (see plant descriptions). An average of 12 hours a day should allow these tubes to last about 6–12 month. The following chart should be used as a rough guide terms of the number of tubes and the wattage based on the size of your aquarium. Deeper aquariums (depth over 45 cm [18 inches]) may require additional wattages depending on the type of plants.

## Lighting Table

Rule of thumb – approximately 1,5 watt per 3,8 l (1 gallon) of water.

### 12 hours of light per day
### Size of Aquarium # Tubes/Wattage

| Size of Aquarium | # | Tubes/Wattage |
|---|---|---|
| 38 l (10 gallon) | 1 | 15 watt tube |
| 57 l (15 gallon) | 1 | 20 watt tube |
| 76 l (20 gallon) | 1 | 30 watt tube |
| 114 l (30 gallon) | 1 | 40 watt tube or |
|  | 2 | 20 watt tubes |
| 152 l (40 gallon) | 2 | 30 watt tubes |
| 190 l (50 gallon*) | 2 | 40 watt tubes |
| 209 l (55 gallon*) | 2 | 40 watt tubes |
| 323 l (85 gallon) | 3 | 40 watt tubes |

* Aquariums over 380 l (100 gallons) double the number of tubes or wattage.

If you cannot ensure daily lighting requirements are met, it is recommended you use an automatic timer to be sure maximized conditions are always present in your aquarium.

Certain plants require more or less lighting than indicated above. These details are included in the information section on idividual plants and tank arrangements.

*Full-spectrum lighting is a must for every natural aquarium.*

## Heating

With the exception of those plants which are only suitable to coldwater environments, tropical plants require continually heated aquariums at an average temperature of about 24° C (75° F). Reliable heater-thermostats are now available from pet shops. Heating "pads", which are buried in the tank substrate, are even better, as they encourage plant growth by warming the plant roots. Tank temperature should be regularly checked using a reliable thermometer.

## Filtration

In the selection of tank filters there are several points of difference between a *natural* and an *artificially* planted aquarium. In an artificially planted aquarium, the determining factors in the selection of a filter are the number, type and size of fish in relationship to the size of the aquarium. In a natural aquarium, the special requirements of plants have to be considered as well. Plants only grow if their roots are in a stable base medium; therefore the use of under-gravel filters may not be desirable in a natural aquarium unless each plant is going to be individually potted. Because of the movement of the water through the gravel created by an undergravel filter, the roots of the plants can be disturbed and may not take hold or grow as they are intended. Therefore a power filter of foam filter is recommended. Another consideration in the selection of the filter is to recognize that most plants benefit from an environment in which their leaves receive strong water circulation. The water returntubes of the filter should be placed in such a way as to provide a current through the leaves of the plants. Simply put, the choice of filters must ensure stability for the roots, and movement and water circulation for the leaves.

Another important consideration is that over vigorous aeration in a natural aquarium should be avoided. Plants consume carbon dioxide and release oxygen. A separate air stone drives carbon dioxide out of the water and increases oxygen. This may disturb the process of photosynthesis. Remember, in all natural aquariums the fish and plants are complementing each other, therefore separate aeration is not required.

*Strong water circulation is very beneficial for the leaves of most aquatic plants.*

# TANK MAINTENANCE FOR PLANTS

## Selecting the base medium

A brief tour of most tropical fish stores creates the accurate impression that there are many gravels, sands or rocks to choose from in laying out the base of an aquarium. In selecting the substrata for a natural aquarium, it is recommended that # 2 or # 3 (about ¹⁄₁₆th–²⁄₁₆th inches) size gravel be used to create the most favorable conditions for aquatic plants to root and prosper.

Planting aquatic plants is very much like planting shrubbery in a yard. Assume that the aquarium gravel and existing yard soil are comparable. For aquatic plants (i.e. ornamental yard shrubs) to properly grow, the gravel (i.e. soil) must be prepared utilizing additional nutrients and fertilizers.

*# 2 or # 3 size gravel forms an ideal substrate for a natural aquarium.*

Such additives are available from most good aquatic shops. Do choose products which come with full instructions for use, and avoid preparations designed for house or garden plants. Be particularly certain that the heater-thermostat that is utilized is reliable and that the water temperature has been raised to approximately 75° F (which is the general range of acceptability for most aquarium plants). As discussed under filtration, strong water circulation at the level of the plant's leaves should be achieved. As a rule of thumb, the filter should be capable of circulating approximately 2–3 times per hour the number of gallons in the aquarium (i.e. a 190 l [50 gallon] aquarium should have a filter capable of circulating the water 570 l [150 gallons] per hour). It is also necessary to measure pH and water hardness to determine which plants should be selected. Reliable complete hardness test and a pH test kits are available from most tropical fish stores.

After proper environment conditions are achieved, your selection of aquatic plants may begin. The descriptions and information of the most popular aquarium plants are provided later. After reading through the different alternatives, it is recommended you develop objectives. These objectives should take into consideration the size of your aquarium and the type of fish you want to keep. If you are trying to develop a replica of an Amazon stream, you will want to carefully read though the section an *Echinodorus*, and you will want to choose fish from this environment. Cardinal and neon tetras, discus and angel fish certainly should be at the top of your list. If your interest is in the quiet streams of Southeast Asia, you certainly will want to look over the outstanding selection of *Cryptocorynes* and consider a barb tank highlighted with a small red-tailed shark or several bala sharks. A coldwater aquarium utilizing *Bacopa* or *Sagittaria* is another alternative. Remember, floating plants such as Java fern and moss are valuable for a bubble-nest-building fish aquarium but they may obscure light essential for rooted plants. Your choices are fascinating and numerous, and do not forget to differentiate among foreground, background and centerpiece plants. These details are well documented for each plant described below.

It is desirable to wait several days after planting your plants before adding your fish. *Tetra* makes two important and distinctly different fertilizers which should be used on a regular basis in maintaining your plants. *Tetra Crypto* is essential to the development and stability of plant roots. Following package instructions, one tablet should be broken and buried in the gravel adjacent to the roots of each plant at first planting and then at every water change to ensure proper growth ingredients are readily availabe.

*Tetra Flora Pride* is an essential fertilizer for the leaves and stems of aquarium plants and compliments *Tetra Crypto*. It should be added to the water initially and with every water change. For Amazon basin aquariums and for soft-water plants in general, *Tetra Spawning Aid* not only creates a favorable environment but its slight tinting effect on the water restrains

*An Amazon Basin aquarium with a variety of Amazon swords and graceful angels. Be sure to select fish which neither "dig" nor eat plant roots.*

the growth of undersired algae on the aquarium glass and rocks. Ask your dealer for further details on these, and other, aquatic plant fertilisers.

## Selecting the fish

In the previous section, some general details were given regarding the types of fish desirable in a natural aquarium. There are some other important considerations.

First, do not select root-eating or root disturbing fish. These include most large cichlids and algae grazers such als *Anostomos, Leporinus* and large barbs, particularly tinfoils. As a general rule, feeding all selected fish in a natural aquarium a supplemental diet of vegetable-based flakes will fulfill their appetite for plants, ensuring that your plants will be relatively undisturbed.

*Tetra* offer books devoted to a pictorial review of the various families and types of aquarium fish. These books are available at most tropical fish stores and give you a full range of fish from the different habitats that can be matched with your selection of aquarium plants. Most good tropical fish dealers will be only too anxious to assist you in your selection. It is important to remember that in a natural aquarium the fish and plants complement one another. Your fish will look better and will be more active as a result and you will achieve far greater enjoyment from your aquarium.

## Maintaining the natural aquarium

Whether your aquarium is natural or utilizes artificial plants, a certain amount of maintenance is required and necessary for its success. This section briefly discusses maintenance practices most suitable for the natural aquarium. Following them assures your natural aquarium will be successful and your fish and plants will prosper.

After the first two weeks from date of original set-up, a very modest 10 to 15% water change is recommended. It is recommended that this water change be made by siphoning the water from the lower third of the aquarium but without disturbing the gravel. Once a month for the first four months approximately 20% of the water should be changed in this manner. On a monthly basis the filter material should be cleaned or replaced. If foam cartridges or foam filter pads in power filters are used, these should be rinsed and squeezed in water the same temperature as that of the aquarium. If wool and charcoal are used, they should be cleaned and changed on an alternating basis; that is the charcoal should be changed one month, the wool changed the next. Although these filter

*Tetra makes a range of gravel washers which should be used when changing water to siphon debris from aquarium gravel. Be sure to maneuver your Hydro-Clean to avoid disturbing plant roots.*

materials are mechanical in that they remove debris from the aquarium water, they are also biological in that they provide surfaces for aerobic or nitrifying bacteria to colonize. These bacteria contribute to the nitrogen cycle in the aquarium. The nitrogen cycle is that important interaction in aquarium life that allows the byproducts of decay, such as fish waste to be broken down from ammonia to nitrites and then to the relatively harmless nitrates which may act as a fertilizer for your plants. After four months, your regular water changes should be made by utilizing a gravel washer to siphon accummulated debris and excess waste materials from the gravel. These can be maneuvered to avoid distrubing plant roots and are much better, and less messy, than ordinary siphons.

With every water change, plant fertiliser should be added following package directions carefully. This will ensure continual development, stability and propagation of most aquatic plants.

Following the guidelines already presented, you should be relatively sure of a successful start to your natural aquarium. Proper lighting, heating and filtration are essential, and regular water testing for hardness pH and nitrite allows you to maintain a stable environment. Fish and plants do best in stable environmental conditions. Develop regular feeding patterns for your fish and follow religiously the maintenance practices already outlined. This will protect against stress to both fish and plants and ensure a successful and rewarding natural aquarium.

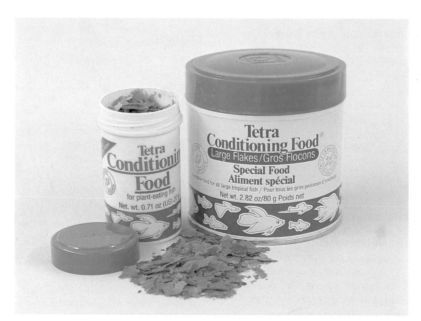

*By feeding fish a supplemental diet of Tetra Conditioning Flakes, their plant requirements are fulfilled and they will be less likely to disturb plants.*

# CARBON DIOXIDE IN THE AQUARIUM

The air around us is not one gas, but a mixture of several. The proportions of the various gases in air are roughly as follows.

Nitrogen ($N_2$)          78%
Oxygen ($O_2$)            21%
Carbon dioxide ($CO_2$)   0.03%
Inert gases               0.93%
Hydrogen ($H_2$)          trace only

The gases carbon dioxide and oxygen are very important in aquarium fishkeeping, their presence and concentration affecting both animal and plant life.

In a well planted tropical freshwater aquarium, the dissolved oxygen level during the daylight hours should be around 8–9 milligrams per litre (mg/l).

This can be confirmed by hobbyists using one of the commercially available dissolved oxygen test kits.

However, if a reading was taken in the same aquarium first thing in the morning, a figure less than the saturation value of 8–9 mg/l would be obtained. This fluctuation is the result of two rather opposing processes, which are:

*Respiration* by the fish and plants (which goes on 24 hours a day), and uses up oxygen and liberates carbon dioxide;

*Photosynthesis* by the plants (which can only take place in bright light), and uses up carbon dioxide and actually liberates oxygen.

Thus in most home aquaria during the daylight hours fish and plants are both using up oxygen, but this is more than compensated for by the photosynthetic activity of the plants. At night (in darkness) plants do not

liberate oxygen but continue (along with the fish) to use it up. These diurnal variations in dissolved oxygen levels also occur in garden ponds, rivers and lakes. As a result of the combined activities of respiration and photosynthesis, dissolved oxygen levels often reach a minimum at about 3–4 am, rising to a maximum at about 1–2 pm.

However, photosynthesis is not the only way in which oxygen can be added to the water. Something like 21% of the air is oxygen. Therefore, water movement (via an airstone or filter) will increase turbulence, which will in turn help dissolve more oxygen into the water. Consequently, adequate aeration/filtration is important in many aquaria, especially those which are densely stocked with fish yet have few plants.

Carbon dioxide is another gas of particular relevance to aquarists. In the average set-up freshwater aquarium, the concentration of carbon dioxide will be as shown below.

| Temperature | | Concentration of carbon dioxide |
|---|---|---|
| °C | °F | (milligrams per litre) |
| 10 | 50 | 0.70 |
| 15 | 59 | 0.60 |
| 20 | 68 | 0.50 |
| 25 | 77 | 0.44 |
| 30 | 86 | 0.38 |

These quantities of carbon dioxide are normally too small for the aquarist to measure. Whenever carbon dioxide is dissolved in water, a small amount of carbonic acid is formed.

*Above: A beautiful planted aquarium.*

$$CO_2 + H_2O = H_2CO_3$$
carbon dioxide + water
= carbonic acid
If the water is alkaline this then dissociates into bicarbonate ($HCO_2$), although under acid conditions most of the bicarbonate is converted back to carbonic acid.

Now, as we are aware, plants require carbon dioxide to grow (as part of the process of photosynthesis mentioned earlier). In fact by increasing carbon dioxide levels, plant growth may be significantly improved. In the aquarium it is possible to add $CO_2$ to the water using commercially available carbon dioxide diffusers. Research at the *Tetra* laboratories in West Germany has shown that if aquarists wish to have a really luxuriant growth of plants in their tanks, they may be well advised to make use of a carbon dioxide diffuser. The carbon dioxide produced by the fish is not enough on its own to stimulate really good plant growth.

## Carbon Dioxide and Aquarium Plants

Therefore, the success of a natural aquarium is very dependent on the balance between carbon dioxide and oxygen. The importance of this correct balance and the photosynthetic process is described in the text of "The Hobbyist Guide to the Natural Aquarium: Comprehensive Edition."
Carbon is an important nutrient for all plants and is absorbed by them in its gaseous state ($CO_2$). While the available

carbon in the atmosphere is almost inexhaustible, this is by no means the case in water. *The Tetra $CO_2$ System* is a practical and very economical means of introducing gaseous $CO_2$ into aquarium water.
An aquarium in which the carbon dioxide equilibrium is correct is very desirable.

– The plants in it will be more vigorous, larger and healthier, because it is only once they have an adequate carbon supply that they are capable of making full use of the other available nutrients.
– $CO_2$ feeding also means that the oxygen content of the water is increased to a marked extent, because the plants are now able to assimilate at an optimum rate.
– The pH value stays within a favorable range which means, for example, that the dangerous ammonia-ammonium reactions that set in at the higher levels, will not now occur.

CO$_2$-concentrations in dependence of pH and KH at 25° C

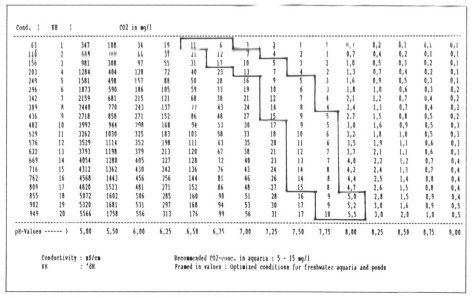

| Cond. | KH | 5,00 | 5,50 | 6,00 | 6,25 | 6,50 | 6,75 | 7,00 | 7,25 | 7,50 | 7,75 | 8,00 | 8,25 | 8,50 | 8,75 | 9,00 |
|---|---|---|---|---|---|---|---|---|---|---|---|---|---|---|---|---|
| 63 | 1 | 347 | 108 | 34 | 19 | 11 | 6 | 3 | 2 | 1 | 1 | 0,1 | 0,2 | 0,1 | 0,1 | 0,1 |
| 110 | 2 | 669 | 198 | 66 | 38 | 21 | 12 | 7 | 4 | 2 | 1 | 0,7 | 0,4 | 0,2 | 0,1 | 0,1 |
| 156 | 3 | 981 | 308 | 97 | 55 | 31 | 17 | 10 | 5 | 3 | 2 | 1,0 | 0,5 | 0,3 | 0,2 | 0,1 |
| 203 | 4 | 1284 | 404 | 128 | 72 | 40 | 23 | 13 | 7 | 4 | 2 | 1,3 | 0,7 | 0,4 | 0,2 | 0,1 |
| 249 | 5 | 1581 | 498 | 157 | 88 | 50 | 28 | 16 | 9 | 5 | 3 | 1,6 | 0,9 | 0,5 | 0,3 | 0,1 |
| 296 | 6 | 1873 | 590 | 186 | 105 | 59 | 33 | 19 | 10 | 6 | 3 | 1,8 | 1,0 | 0,6 | 0,3 | 0,2 |
| 342 | 7 | 2159 | 681 | 215 | 121 | 68 | 38 | 21 | 12 | 7 | 4 | 2,1 | 1,2 | 0,7 | 0,4 | 0,2 |
| 389 | 8 | 2440 | 770 | 243 | 137 | 77 | 43 | 24 | 14 | 8 | 4 | 2,4 | 1,3 | 0,7 | 0,4 | 0,2 |
| 436 | 9 | 2718 | 858 | 271 | 152 | 86 | 48 | 27 | 15 | 9 | 5 | 2,7 | 1,5 | 0,8 | 0,5 | 0,2 |
| 482 | 10 | 2992 | 944 | 298 | 168 | 94 | 53 | 30 | 17 | 9 | 5 | 3,0 | 1,6 | 0,9 | 0,5 | 0,3 |
| 529 | 11 | 3262 | 1030 | 325 | 183 | 103 | 58 | 33 | 18 | 10 | 6 | 3,2 | 1,8 | 1,0 | 0,5 | 0,3 |
| 576 | 12 | 3529 | 1114 | 352 | 198 | 111 | 63 | 35 | 20 | 11 | 6 | 3,5 | 1,9 | 1,1 | 0,6 | 0,3 |
| 622 | 13 | 3793 | 1198 | 379 | 213 | 120 | 67 | 38 | 21 | 12 | 7 | 3,7 | 2,1 | 1,1 | 0,6 | 0,3 |
| 669 | 14 | 4054 | 1280 | 405 | 227 | 128 | 72 | 40 | 23 | 13 | 7 | 4,0 | 2,2 | 1,2 | 0,7 | 0,4 |
| 716 | 15 | 4312 | 1362 | 430 | 242 | 136 | 76 | 43 | 24 | 14 | 8 | 4,2 | 2,4 | 1,3 | 0,7 | 0,4 |
| 762 | 16 | 4568 | 1443 | 456 | 256 | 144 | 81 | 46 | 26 | 14 | 8 | 4,4 | 2,5 | 1,4 | 0,8 | 0,4 |
| 809 | 17 | 4820 | 1523 | 481 | 271 | 152 | 86 | 48 | 27 | 15 | 8 | 4,7 | 2,6 | 1,5 | 0,8 | 0,4 |
| 855 | 18 | 5072 | 1602 | 506 | 285 | 160 | 90 | 51 | 28 | 16 | 9 | 5,0 | 2,8 | 1,5 | 0,9 | 0,4 |
| 902 | 19 | 5320 | 1681 | 531 | 297 | 168 | 94 | 53 | 30 | 17 | 9 | 5,2 | 3,0 | 1,6 | 0,9 | 0,5 |
| 949 | 20 | 5566 | 1758 | 556 | 313 | 176 | 99 | 56 | 31 | 17 | 10 | 5,5 | 3,0 | 2,0 | 1,0 | 0,5 |

pH-Values ------ )

Conductivity : µS/cm
KH : °dH

Recommended CO2-conc. in aquaria : 5 - 15 mg/l
Framed in values : Optimized conditions for freshwater aquaria and ponds

*(provided by Dr. Ritter Chemical R & D of Tetra)*

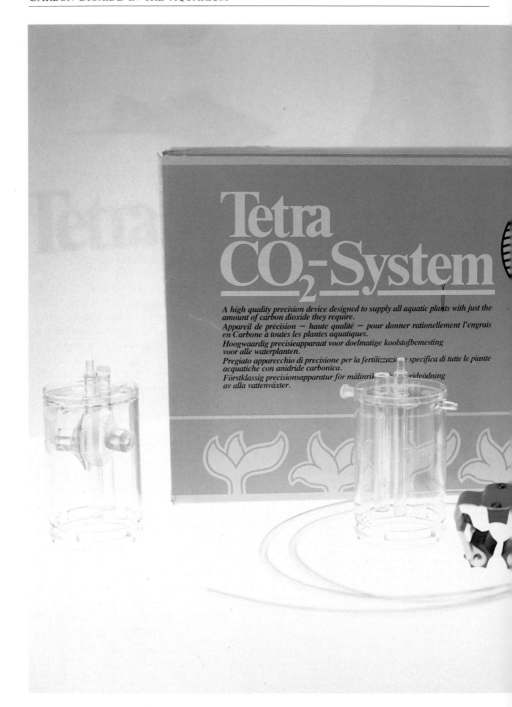

To determine if the $CO_2$ concentration is correct, periodic water testing of pH and carbon hardness is recommended. The chart shows the optimum $CO_2$ concentrations at a temperature of 77° F (25° C), based on the correlation of pH and kH (carbonate hardness).

Of some importance in a consideration of carbon dioxide in the aquarium, is the buffering capacity (ie. carbonate hardness, KH) of the water. The presence of carbonate hardness prevents marked shifts of pH when carbon dioxide is added to the aquarium. The bicarbonates ($HCO_3$) of the carbonate hardness effectively "mop up" the carbon dioxide resulting in the formation of very little carbonic acid. However, in water with no carbonate hardness (or when the buffering capacity becomes exhausted), the addition of carbon dioxide may cause a significant drop in pH, which may harm the fish. Therefore, if you are contemplating improving your plant growth by the use of a carbon dioxide diffuser, the carbonate hardness of the water should be measured using a reliable test kit. Depending on the KH value of the water, the

◀ *Tetra CO₂-System*

following amounts of carbon dioxide may then be added. KH value below 2° dH –
up to 15 mg/l of carbon dioxide
KH value 2 to 10° dH –
up to 20 mg/l of carbon dioxide
KH value above 10° dH –
up to 30 mg/l of carbon dioxide

It should be noted that exposure of fish to a concentration of carbon dioxide of 40 mg/l (or more) for an extended period may lead to problems (ie. lack of vitality, reduced resistance to disease). The commercially available carbon dioxide diffusers should come with some form of calibration which allows the amount of carbon dioxide added to the aquarium to be measured. A word of warning: it is rather dangerous to use an ordinary carbon dioxide cylinder connected to an air-stone, rather than a proper aquarium carbon dioxide diffuser. In the former instance, the level of carbon dioxide in the aquarium is difficult to control, which may result in excessively high levels and dangerously low pH values.

A few hobbyists will be familiar with the term "biogenic decalcfication". If there is a lack of carbon dioxide in the water, some plants are able to effectively remove it from bicarbonates of the KH.

The carbon dioxide is removed and calcium carbonate deposited as a white precipitate, often on the leaves of the plants. This chemical reaction causes the pH to rise, and the water becomes more alkaline. The above reaction is reversible, and if carbon dioxide were added to the water the pH would then fall, and the calcium carbonate would go back into solution as calcium bicarbonate.

Remember that overvigorous aeration in a luxuriantly planted, natural aquarium, with tend to drive off carbon dioxide which could be used by the plants. The aim is to establish a balance between fish and plants – hence the term a "natural aquarium".

*A natural aquarium – balance between fish and plants.*

# CABOMBA AND SIMILAR PLANTS

In selecting aquatic plants there are certain species that are especially easy to cultivate in an aquarium . . . as well as those with special requirements making them very difficult. The cultivation of the majority of stemmed plants, however, does not offer many difficulties. They adapt themselves within a few days to a new tank and grow rapidly within a short period of time if the water conditions are correct. In fact, their rate of growth may be so rapid that the aquarist may frequently have to trim roots. It is just this rapid growth that is needed in an aquarium in order to obtain healthy conditions for a favorable "plant environment". To maintain this growth rate, many stemmed plants depend on leaf fertilisation (ie. absorbing nutrients through their leaves). Therefore, for these varieties regular additions of liquid plant fertiliser to the water is absolutely essential. A few stemmed plants, however, are not as easy to cultivate. Some require lots of light for the development of their leaves fresh green color, for instance *Cabomba aquatica*. In general stemmed plants require more light than a group of cryptocorynes. There is one remarkable observation: in their native habitat many of these plants are marsh plants. Like many other aquarium plants, they have been selected for total underwater life by aquarists. Some stemmed plants, reverting to natural inclinations, have a tendency to grow beyond the surface of the water. This can easily be avoided by trimming the shoots. In general, stemmed plants grow easily and rapidly and the aquarist will enjoy trimming them

back. Culturing stemmed plants is very satisfying as the shoots are easily cultivated when planted as cuttings.

## Bacopa caroliniana
*Native Habitat:*
Southeast North America

This is a stout, fleshy-leaved plant ideal for all aquariums. Its leaves have a round to oval form which sometimes reach a length of almost 2 cm (1 inch). In nature, *Bacopa* is a marsh plant and therefore it does not grow extremely rapidly in aquariums. *Bacopa* should be planted in small groups, with strong illumination, in either the back or aquarium center. In larger tanks this plant is very decorative when planted in groups directly in front as a foreground planting. This plant naturally grows out above the surface of the water, and will flower profusely in the aquarium if there is sufficient space between the water and cover glass, and even if fully submerged. The attractive blue/violet flowers are bell shaped and are produced on long stalks. *Bacopas*, if trimmed, are well-suited for smaller aquaria, too. Because of its native North American origin, no special temperatures are required. *Bacopa* is easily acclimated to life on cold water or tropical tanks and thrive in both relatively hard and soft water. The most important factor for this plant species is strong light.

A similar species, *B. monnieri*, has slim leaves and is a more delicate plant. Its native habitat is tropical and subtropical America. Both species can easily be reproduced by planting cuttings. In rather shallow tanks they have the tendency to grow up beyond the water surface.

## Cabomba (Various species)
*Native Habitat:*
Warm Regions of North and South America

The delicate shining green leaves of the *Cabomba* species make them one of the most decorative stem plants. Unfortunately, they are one of the most demanding species with regard to light requirements. In order to obtain very strong cuttings, very intense illumination is required. It is recommended to install one or two additional fluorescent tubes, especially if the water depth is more than 50 cm (20 inches).

While most *Cabomba* need soft water, especially *C. aquatica*, water of medium hardness is equally suited as long as the aquarist follows the tank practices outlined earlier.

Quite a number of different *Cabomba* are commonly available. The most common are the North American *C. caroliniana* and its many varieties. This species is relatively easy to keep. *C. piauhyensis* (native habitat Central and Northern South America) keeps its brown-reddish dye if the lighting is intense enough. The most delicate and most beautiful of all the *Cabomba* species is *C. aquatica*. The best conditions for optimal growth are soft water and peat filtration, as well as added fertilization, and an intense illumination. *C. aquatica* surpasses all other aquatic plants with regard to beauty. It should be kept at 72°–80° F (22 to 26° C), while *C. caroliniana* is less delicate with respect to water temperatures. As with all other stem plants, the question arises whether to trim the shoots or to take the plant out of the aquarium to cut the rootstock and then replant them. The cutting and re-planting method is better since trimmed plants do not look good, especially if the new shoots or branches may fail to grow.

*Above Top: Bacopa caroliniana*
*Above Left: Bacopa monnieri with flower*
*Above Right: Bacopa caroliniana with flower*
*Right: Cabomba species are attractive plants, but they often need soft water and quite high light levels.*

plants in a tank is not easily accomplished and is best avoided.

Provided the plants grow rapidly, all *Egeria* species are effective producers of oxygen and are ideally suited for densely populated aquariums. They even thrive at high pH-values 7.2–7.8. *Elodea canadensis* is suited for cold water tanks only.

**Heteranthera zosterfolia**
*Native Habit:*
Tropical South-America

For more than 70 years this species has been the favorite among all *Heteranthera* imports due to the simple culturing and the decorative value. Effective illumination is required in order to keep the plants from becoming lean and thin-leaved. *Heteranthera* is especially suited for small shallow tanks. It looks best when arranged in groups, which is true for all stem plants. *Heteranthera* grow very rapidly when cultivated under proper conditions; they do not have the tendency to grow above the water surface. A regular partial change of water is important, the hardness degree of

**Egeria densa** (Elodea densa)
*Native Habitat:*
Argentina

In general this species adapts itself very easily and is therefore well-suited for the new as well as advanced aquarist. The species thrives even at temperatures of 68° F (20° C) provided there is good illumination and water that is not too soft. If *E. densa* is shaded by other plants or if the illumination is poor, stems become thin and the attractive appearance deteriorates. It is best to plant this species in the back or the middle of the tank. Water depth should be approximately 40 cm (16 inches). Full-spectrum lighting should be present, with the temperature range of 68°–75° F (20°–24° C). To arrange *E. densa* with other

*Heteranthera zosterifolia*

the water is not, although it is recommended to soften extremely hard water. Shoots of this species build a rich root system; therefore it is very advisable to add a suitable fertiliser to the gravel regularly.

## Hygrophila difformis
*Native Habitat:*
From India to the Malayan Peninsula
The species, formerly known as *Synnema triflorum* is one of the most favored aquatic plants because it is remarkably attractive. It also grows extremely well when cultivated under appropriate conditions.
Single shoots may be planted in small tanks where the vividly shining roseshaped leaves beautifully contrast the dark green

*Hygrophila difformis*

of cryptocryones. The best appearance, however, can be obtained when *Hygrophila difformis* is planted (arranged) in groups in lager tanks. The stems should be arranged closely together. The planting itself is not difficult. When the shoots are planted close together the roots develop rather rapidly. Plants that are deeply rooted sometimes grow small roots on top of the bottom material. Culturing is restricted to trimming.
This species does not have the tendency to grow beyond the water surface, and adapts itself very rapidly and without doubt is a most attractive plant. To maintain this plant, full illumination and regular water changes are a must. It is important also to keep the temperature at 75° F (24° C). This species will thrive in soft to medium hard water.

## Hygrophila polysperma
*Native Habitat:*
Southeast Asia
*Hygrophila polysperma* is one of the most popular and best-known aquatic plants. It is a good background plant; in larger tanks it may be grouped in the middle.
The shining green color of the leaves contrasts the dark colored leaves of cryptocoryne groups. Small compact groups of *Hygrophila polysperma* are especially effective. In general this plant is considered extremely accomodating; this, however, should not be taken for granted. Good illumination is required in order to obtain a bushy, decorative, strong growth. Avoid shadowing by large, broad-leaved plants. Although this plant can stand an occasional lowering of the temperature without any danger, the optimal growth rate can be obtained between 70°–82° F (22 to 28° C). *Hygrophila polysperma* acclimates to water conditions for most aquatic plants and will prosper if the aquarium is established and maintained as described earlier.

*Hygrophila polysperma*

## Hydrocotyle leucocephala
*Native Habitat:*
Tropical South America
This plant is similar in structure to the European *H. vulgaris*, but is hardier and grows more rapidly. *Hydrocotyle leucocephala* does not creep on the tank bottom but grows *only* upwards. This species is an excellent foreground plant with its diagonally-growing bright green shoots. No other requirements than those already described are necessary. The temperature should be constantly maintained between 72°–75° F (22–25° C). Occasionally trimming is needed. *Hydrocotyle leucocephala* is suitable for all size aquariums and it is becoming more common in the aquarium trade. This attractive plant resembles a cluster of small umbrellas that are stacked one upon the other. It gives the aquarium an almost oriental appearance.

The bright green leaves provide an excellent contrast to any dark background. No matter whether planted individually or in groups, the effect is the same.

*Hydrocotyle leucocephala*

The character of the plant changes as it grows. When provided with bright illumination it soon reaches the water surface. From this time on, the rooted stem grows weaker, losing leaf after leaf, until it dies. The pennywort thus develops into a floating plant.

Runners branch out across the water surface until the entire surface is covered. This carpet, with its fine roots, can provide protection and food for young fish. Occasionally, pennywort takes on the characteristics of a bog plant, attempting to sprout above the surface.

Pennywort may be propagated by taking cuttings from either the rootstock or the floating runners. These should be planted on the bottom where they will soon develop, striving to reach the surface.

## Hydrocotyle vulgaris
*Native Habitat:*
Europe

The European pennywort does not have an erect stem but rather its stems grow by „creeping" on the tank bottom. This is exclusively a foreground plant; a small group in a larger tank is of highly decorative value. This is mostly due to the extraordinary form of the leaves, which are almost perfectly round, borne on more or less slender stems. In Europe, *Hydrocotyle vulgaris* grows more or less naturally in marsh land, tolerating occasional floods. This adaptability is useful in a tank. Some aquarists are successful in their first attempt: they manage to keep *H. vulgaris* for a long period of time in a tropical tank and it does not lose its attraction. In other tanks the stems tend to elongate and the leaves become smaller and smaller until the plant dies. Important in order to obtain lasting success is the following: an acid tank, bottom fertilized regularly, and very good illumination. Temperatures should not be too high (maximum 77° F or 25° C) and the pH-value should not exeed 6.5.

*Hydrocotyle vulgaris*

31

*Above: Limnophila aquatica*

*Below: Limnophila sessiliflora*

**Limnophila** (Various species)
*Native Habitat:*
Tropical Southeast Asia

At first sight, the *Limnophila species* look like *Cabomba*; it is, however, easy to tell the difference. With *Limnophila* the different sections of the leaves are arranged regularly in circle form around the stem (see picture). Apart from that all *Limnophila* species are just as beautiful as *Cabomba*; they are, however, not quite as demanding with regard to their surroundings. But they must be placed in full light in order to develop a beautiful rich growth.

This plant should be planted in large groups in order to obtain a striking effect. Also *L. sessiliflora* may become the center of attraction in a tank when planted in groups. This species is commonly available. The whorl of leaves may reach a diameter of approximately 5 cm (2 inches). Due to the beautiful and stout appearance, this species is one of the most attractive aquatic plants. Relatively new is *L. aquatica* from Sri Lanka, the *"giant Limnophila"*, whose whorl may reach a diameter of up to 12 cm (4½ inches). Therefore this plant is only recommended for large tanks. This species cannot be cultivated by cuttings; cultivation occurs only through the formation of the roots and new shoots. All *Limnophila* species should be trimmed regularly (see *Cabomba*). Fertilization and regular water change guarantees a continual gorgeous plant growth.

**Lobelia cardinalis**
*Native Habitat:* North America
At first glance, this aquatic plant resembles *Nomaphila* (see below); however, it does

*Lobelia cardinalis*

not reach the size of the latter. In spite of its North American origin, where it grows in wet meadows as a marsh plant, it may be kept in the tropical aquarium. Here it is handled just the same as *Nomaphila*. In view of the fact that this species is, in general, a little smaller, it forms beautiful shining green plant groups in medium lage tanks. There are no special requirements other than the basic procedures already outlined. A less agreeable characteristic of this species is that it grows up beyond the water surface; even more so than the *Nomaphila* species. The aquarist has to make sure that he regularly trims the shoots which in turn leads to increased branching. In case the stems are bare, new cuttings will have to be planted.

**Ludwigia** (Various species)
*Native Habitat:*
Almost worldwide
There are a number of plant species available under the name of *Ludwigia*.

*Ludwigia species*

Most often they are *Ludwigia repens*, whose native habitat is Middle America as well as South America and the Caribbean. It has many varieties; including a cross breeding between *L. repens* and *L. palustris*, known as "*L. mullertii*", an increasingly popular and well-known aquatic plant. Due to the reddish dye of the underside of the leaves this *Ludwigia* is especially attractive. Often the entire plant shows a reddish dye. Unfortunately, this color does not last long under poor illumination, but apart from that it is well-suited for tanks. There are no special requirements with regard to temperature. It needs, however, very intensive illumination, significantly more than other stem plants. The distance between the above tank light and the tank bottom should be kept as short as possible. The aquarist should not use a deep tank for this species.

**Myriophyllum** (Various species)
*Native Habitat*:
Worldwide
*Myriophyllum* are beautiful, unmistakable aquatic plants. With their hairlike, segmented leaves they have a characteristic shape. Their best properties – beauty and adaptability – develop only in cold water tanks, at high light intensity and water temperatures not exceeding 75° F (24° C). This temperature is best for species from moderate climates, preferably North American species such as *M. hippuroides*, which grows gorgeously and tolerates temperatures up to 75° F (24° C). The European species are less suited for tropical tank life. They should be cultured exclusively in cold water aquaria.
From the tropical part of America originates *M. aquaticum*, which is called "parrot's feather" because of the shape of the leaves. This species needs a good illumination and warm water. Unfortunately, it does not reach the beauty and abundancy of the "cold water species". Presently there are

*Myriophyllum aquatica*

*Myriophyllum mattogrossense*

other tropical species available as well including *M. mattogrossense*, which thrives in tropical tanks. While the *Myriophyllum* species may be kept in the tropical aquarium as well (and they look very beautiful), they always remain just "guests" in warm water tanks as they are not easily accommodating to tropical surroundings. It is important for all *Myriophyllum* species that the aquarium water is kept very still; bottom feeders should be avoided. Dirt particles collect in the hair-like leaves, which not only looks unattractive but stops the plant growth. There are no special requirements with respect to the bottom material and water chemistry.

**Najas** (Various species)
*Native Habitat:*
Tropical and semi tropical regions
Most of the time it is difficult to distinguish a genuine *Naja microdon* from its many look alikes. With their fine linear, almost 2 cm (1 inch) long and only 1 mm (¼ inch) thick and leaves that grow very close together. *Najas* are a very attractive plant, just as *Myriophyllum*. They are often used as spawning plants. It is astonishing how rapidly *Najas* grow. Often the aquarist is forced to trim the plants once a week. Many hobbyists try to plant them in groups. This is difficult as the stems break very easily and the roots often do not deve-

*Najas species*

lop. When planted in groups, however, *Najas* may be a decorative contrast to other plants, especially in small tanks. Other hobbyists treat *Najas* "the way nature does", leaving them freefloating on the surface of the tank water. The shining green color of the leaves contrasts impressively when seen from "underwater" through the bright light of the fluorescent tubes. *Najas* do not have to be planted; they live free-floating and take all the nutritive substances they require from the water. The aquarist should pay attention to this fact when changing the water by adding fertilisers very sparingly.

## Nomaphila stricta
*Native Habitat:*
Southeast Asia
*Nomaphila* is suited only for large tanks due to its giant size (leaf length approximately 8 cm, 3 inches). In a large tank this

species might be planted as a single plant, or according to the tank size, as a background plant. When rooted in gravel, the cuttings of this plant grow very rapidly. Sometimes this species loses its upper leaves immediately, which is due to a disturbance of its metabolism; this can be avoided by changing the tank water more frequently. Stripped stems should be trimmed and used as cuttings. *Nomaphila* has no special requirements with regard to water temperature and water conditions. The aquarist should bear in mind, however, that this species requires intense illumination without shade.

## Rotala macrandra (top right)
*Native Habitat:*
India
This species is one of the most popular novelties of the recent years. Just a glance

*Nomaphila stricta*

at the color photo picture conveys it is a beautiful plant with brillant colors. Compared with *Rotala rotundifolia* this plant looks more like a *Ludwigia*. As with many other "red" aquatic plants it is necessary to make certain restrictions regarding the brilliant colors since the wonderful reddish dye will fade away or turn into a reddish olive-green when this plant is exposed to poor illumination. The reddish dye is best preserved by supplementing fullspectrum lighting with a short-wave blue fluorescent lamp. *Rotala macrandra* really enriches the aquarium. Since this species grows rapidly and distinguishes itself by growing numerous auxillary shoots, only a few cuttings are needed to grow a real bush, which after some time may grow up to 40 cm (16 inches) in height.

As an exception from the rule the trimming of the plant's shoots has a very favorable effect: it induces branching. *Rotala* stays in excellent form in water with a pH-value of 6.8, with partial changing every week, and peat filtering. Special light requirement: two full-spectrum fluorescent tubes and one blue fluorescent lamp.

**Rotala rotundifolia** (below)
*Native Habitat:*
Southeast Asia

During recent years this species has become more and more popular, especially in small tanks. This is a stem plant and is ideal in decorative groups with its elongated, lanceolated brillant green leaves that have a slightly reddish dye at the top and are scarcely 1.5 cm (½ inch) long. Also, it will lighten up the foreground in large tanks. Shading by other plants, however, should be avoided. With regard to cultivation, this species accommodates itself very easily and it may be kept in a tank for a long time. It does not grow rapidly. In free nature it is a marsh plant; in tanks, however, it never shows the tendency to grow beyond the water surface.

# VALLISNERIA AND OTHER SIMILAR PLANTS

In addition to stemmed plants there should be rosette plants in any underwater landscape. To select from, there are the large groups of cryptocorynes with their many varieties; the swordplants (*Echinodorus*), and others with a more grass-like appearance. One of these, *Vallisneria spiralis* has for decades been a permanent reserve in nearly all aquariums. This plant, as well as *Sagittaria* (both have a similar appearance), should be planted in groups since it does not produce any effect when planted alone. The group planting renders this species useful for covering (masking) the sides and the back of the tank. There are different species for different tank sizes: from dwarf *Sagittaria* to make the "foreground lawn" to the giant *Vallisneria* whose measurements surpass the dimensions of most aquariums.

*Vallisneria species*

## Acorus gramineus var. pusillus

*Native Habitat:*

East Asia

The dwarf form of *Acorus gramineus* with its bushy, grass like, stiff leaves, which are about 5–7 cm (2–3 inches) long, and its strong rhizome, is a very delicate and beautiful aquatic plant Nevertheless, there are certain restrictions with regard to its durability in a tropical tank. This plant grows best in very shallow water. If it is kept submerged, the temperature should not be too high, approximately 50°–68° F (15–20° C). This plant should be exposed to full illumination. *A. gramineus* is a very beautiful foreground plant, which should be planted in small thick groups. In a tropical tank, these plants have to be replaced frequently as their appearance deteriorates after some time. Apart from green variations, there exists another with bright stripes. This species is even more frequently found on the market than the green dwarf form.

## Samolus valerandi

*Native Habitat:*

America, Tropical and Moderate Regions

This small delicate plant with its shining pale-green leaves, which are 5–6 cm (2–3 inches) long and show a rosette form of growth. Originally it was a marsh plant, which to a certain degree has adapted itself to the conditions of a tank. Of special attraction is the delicate form of the leaf rosettes. *Samolus* is the ideal foreground plant. The aquarist has to buy several plants at a time, as proliferation takes place only under very favorable circumstances. This species should be grouped closely together. For successful cultivation, intense, full spectrum light is necessary and the tubes must be installed close together. It is important that the tank is not deeper than 30 cm (12 inches). *Samolus* will thrive in a firm, fertile substrate; therefore the aquarist must use a gravel fertiliser. This species is suited for cold water tanks; in a tropical tank it is less prolific.

## Vallisneria spiralis

*Native Habitat:*

Southern Europe, Subtropical and Tropical Regions (Origin of individual species uncertain)

*Vallisneria* is one of the oldest and most well-known aquarium plants. It was mentioned at the end of the 19th century in literature dealing with the aquatic hobby.

From a botanically point of view. *Vallisneria* should belong to the stem plants. Its

*Vallisneria corkscrew –*
*Vallisneria asiatica*

"stems", however, are hidden horizontally in the substratum, bearing those grass-like rosettes which we call the plant. With its long, linear, pale to middle-green leaves, which may reach 50 cm (20 inches) in length, *Vallisneria* is an especially valuable aquatic plant. The size of the leaves, however, restricts its use to large aquaria only. It really does not look good when the long leaves bend when reaching the surface of the water. This also has the effect of shading the other plants. The bottom material should be fertilised, which will induce the production of runners. Good illumination will help the plants to grow. *Vallisneria* has a much more extensive range of temperature tolerance than similar *Sagittaria* species.

*Vallisneria* may be left entirely to themselves if there is plenty of room and when grouped as background plants. Due to the reproduction by runners they build a good stock over time. Offsets may be detached from their parents and replanted if the new plants develop in an unsuitable direction. *Vallisneria* is extremely accommodating in respect to temperature. There is no danger even if the water temperature goes down to 50° F (12° C). In a balanced, well-run tank it is possible to watch a flower on a long thin stalk, growing to the surface of the water. Fertilization, however, takes place only if "male" plants are in the tank, too.

*Vallisneria spiralis* has dwarf varieties as well as those which grow larger. Their exact indentification is often uncertain. Stout, horticultural varieties with twisted leaves belong to *Vallisneria asiatica var. biwaensis*. It should be used as a single plant or in small groups centered in the middle of the tank as an eye-catcher *Vallisneria asiatica* with its strongly twisted leaves (approximately 30 cm (12 inches) remains smaller than *Vallisneria spiralis*. In soft water *Vallisneria spiralis* does not thrive well. Medium hard water should be used.

**Vallisneria gigantea**
*Native Habitat:*
New Guinea, Philippines
At first glance this species looks like *Vallisneria spiralis*, but its linear leaves are considerably longer, up to 2 m (6 feet) and 3 cm (1¼ inches) wide. If the aquarist really wants to cultivate a plant of this size he needs a tank of at least 380 l (100 gallons),

*Vallisneria gigantea*

otherwise it will never look good. All plants offered as giant *Vallisneria* may not be *giant Vallisneria* but cross-breedings between *Vallisneria spiralis* and *Vallisneria gigantea*. The growth rate of these crosses makes this plant suitable for medium sized tanks. In very large tanks *Vallisneria gigantea* should be used as a background plant or as a solitary group (3–4 single plants are very decorative). The tank, however, should not be too shallow so that the leaves may expand freely. The cross-breedings between *Vallisneria gigantea* and *Vallisneria spiralis* need higher temperatures, 68°–86° F (20–30° C), than *V. spiralis*.

**Sagittaria platyphylla**
*Native Habitat:*
North America
With its stout, linear leaves which can grow up to a length of up to 30 cm (12 inches), this plant resembles a giant *Vallisneria*. *Sagittaria platyphylla* always remains a little bit shorter and is therefore suited for medium sized tanks. In order to obtain broad, strong, intensively green foliage, this species has to be exposed to full illumination. Regular use of aquarium fertiliser is important for this plant. *S. platyphylla* is extremely accommodating in respect to water temperatures; it will thrive in cold water as well as in tropical tanks.
*Sagittaria subulata* has smaller leaves. It is, however, difficult to see the distinguishing characteristics when these plants are submerged. A very popular variety, similar to *Echinodorus tenellus*, is called *S. subulata*

*forma pusilia*, the dwarf form. When exposed to full illumination in shallow tanks, all *Sagittaria* grow floating leaves. This indicates that they are *Sagittaria* and not *Vallisneria* which do not grow such leaves. These two species are often confused as they look very much alike. A clear distinguishing feature is the following: the longitudinal veins of the *Vallisnerias* leaf end in its tip, while the *Sagittaria* species show veins that end before the tip on the edge of the leaf and can only be seen with a magnifying glass.

*Sagittaria platyphylla*

# CRYPTOCORYNES IN THE WILD AND THE AQUARIUM

There is no other aquatic plant which combines the two valuable characteristics of extraordinary beauty and extreme suitability to aquarium conditions as well as cryptocorynes. As a result, cryptocorynes are very popular and well-known among aquarists. In view of these facts, cryptocorynes are just "made for the aquarium". They are the world's most popular and best known aquatic plants! As "character plants" of Southeast Asian origin they should be in every "South Asia tank" (i.e. any aquarium with barbs)

To maximize the beauty, growth, and full development of cryptocorynes the practices outlined earlier in this book should be followed. Cryptocorynes are extremely sensitive to environmental changes such as temperature, build up of waste, and decreases in lighting.

Cryptocorynes also do not like a frequent replanting. Few interruptions and disturbances will ensure that cryptocorynes thrive. Many will even thrive in hard water at approximately 11° dH (general hardness). It is recommended to check the pH-value of the water if cryptocorynes are cultivated. By peat filtration and by adding *Spawning Aid*, a growth-promoting environment is enhanced. The number of the different species, cultivated in aquariums today is remarkable. The shapes and growth forms differ considerably. Your dealer's standard stock offers cryptocorynes for every tank and purpose: small foreground plants such as *C. willisii*; varieties that will grow larger for planting in the

middle or back, up to the almost giant *C. ciliata*. Although all cryptocorynes have approximately the same requirements (except *C. ciliata*), when cultivated there are varieties among them which distinguish themselves by a rapid growth or the producing of runners. Other varieties are rather "lazy" with regard to these two characteristics.

The varieties mentioned on the following pages are mostly rapidly growing and very accommodating, easy to cultivate and well-suited for the different methods of planting and decorating. When planting, the aquarist should make sure that cryptocorynes are not rooted too deeply (the crown should be visible). All cryptocorynes propagate by runners.

## Cryptocorynes in the wild

In our attempts at growing a number of water plants from Malaysia in our tanks, we are faced with certain problems. We do not know, for instance, why *Cryptocoryne nurii* or *C. schulzei* grow so poorly in aquaria or why the magnificent *Barclaya motleyi* or *B. rotundifolia* are practically a total failure. In their natural habitat they grow profusely and multiply plentifully by means of runners. In addition, we are faced with problems of nomenclature. The systematics of the *Cryptocoryne* genus is very difficult because they can only be identified by the shape and color of the flower the leaf form and size etc, all of which can be very variable. For instance, a totally distinct type of cryptocoryne was being distributed in Europe under the name *C. cordata*. In some aquarium literature we read that the collar of the spathe (the spathe is the leaf-like sheath enveloping the flower) of *C. cordata* is purple. This is incorrect, for *C. cordata* has, in fact a bright yellow collar (see below). All the problems of propagation and nomenclature can only be solved by on the spot investigation, and so recently went on a field trip to western Malaysia.

The west coast of the Malayan peninsula between Johore, Bahru, Malacca and Kuala Lumpur is not particularly interesting from the point of view of the aquarist. The road is bordered by an un-ending series of rubber or oil-palm plantations. The original rain forest has been totally destroyed to make way for these

*Cryptocoryne cordata, and the yellow collar to the flower.*

plantations. The water courses are now more or less regulated and usually subject to the full glare of the sun. The only crypto-coryne we found here was *C. ciliata*, though there were *Blyxa echinosperma*, *Limnophila indica*, *Eleocharis* and *Utricularia*.

The swamps along the road were covered with water hyacinths, *Eichhornia crassipes*. This floating plant was introduced and the governments of the Malayan Federation and of Singapore prohibit the raising of what has now become a water weed and a nuisance. However the economic value of these plants is high as they are used as fodder for all sorts of domestic animals and so the ruling is scarcely ever observed in reality.

Only East Johore between Jemaluang-Kahang and Jemuluang Kota Tinggi is a genuine cryptocoryne paradise and may be thought of as the "promised land" for catching aquarium fish. The surroundings in this area are vast expanses of primeval, usually swampy, rain forest just the sort of area to investigate for unusual fish or aquatic plants.

Our first collecting trips in Johore took us to the Jemaluang-Kangkar Kahang district where the plants found growing included *Cryptocoryne nurii* and *C. schulzei* and both types of *Barclaya, B. montleyi* and *B. rotundifolia*. The first locality where we found cryptocorynes was a few miles behind Jemaluang. With the exception of Sungei Kahang, all the water courses that crossed the road were really just small forest streams. They were 2–4 m (6–12 feet) wide and their depth varied from 10–20 cm (4–8 inches) near the bank where the water is faster flowing to 7.5 cm (3 inches) in still water pools. These measurements were taken at the beginning of May. At this time the south west monsoon carries the rain to the west coast. I was

*The neutral home of the crytocarynes.* ▷

*Carpet of plants of Cryptocoryne nuri in small stream in the rain forest.*

making my observations on the east coast which had dry, sunny weather. We searched in many streams as far as Kangkar Kahang and found thick carpets of cryptocorynes in nearly all of them. The plants grew here in abundance, thousands of them side by side! It is interesting to note that *Cryptocoryne nurii* and *C. schulzei* never grow together. In some streams we found the one variety, in others the second, but always isolated from one another. Later, north of Kota Tinggi, I found *C. cordata* and *C. schulzei*, together in one locality on infrequent occasions, but it was very rare to find these two species of cryptocoryne together on one site.

*Barclaya motleyi* and *B. rotundifolia* grew throughout the whole of this area but they did not occur together with cryptocorynes. We found them sporadically, but only where the water was more than 20 cm (8 inches) deep. They never formed the thick leafy carpets characteristic of the cryptocorynes.

All varieties of cryptocorynes and *Barclaya* in Johore (with the exception of *Cryptocoryne ciliata*) always preferred intensely shaded waters in forested areas. They were only rarely found in streams that flowed through more open rubber plantations. But even when they occured here they grew in shady sites.

If we were to discover why *Cryptocoryne nurii, C. schulzei* and both species of *Barclaya* a grow so poorly in our aquaria, we had familiarise ourselves with their natural conditions and make changes accordingly in our tanks at home.

We first considered the water quality, particularly its color. The water in the cryptocoryne habitat was clear, but it was coloured brownish to dark reddish brown as a result of added humic acids which give the water its extremely acidic character. In all the measurements that I carried out, the pH value was around 4.8. The general hardness was below 1° dH (i.e. very soft).

It was noticeable that a thick layer of a brownish sediment lay covering the carpet of leaves. If we looked down on to the stream from a bridge, we sometimes had no idea that there were great expanses of plants growing below us. It was only on wading into the water that we could see that we were standing in the midst of cryptocorynes. At first I was of the opinion that ferric hydroxide made up the greater part of this sediment. We could explain the increased iron content in the water by the reddish-brown soil. But the water analyses showed that the iron content in the water was about 1.4 mg/l. This figure is indeed relatively high but such levels also occur in our own peaty waters in Germany. The sediment on the cryptocoryne leaves was to be mostly of a clayloamy mud. Apart from the iron, I was also interested by the ammonia and nitrate contents, which are also important nitrogenous nutrients for plants. It turned out that cryptocoryne waters in Johore were very unproductive only contained low levels of total ammonia, less than 0.05 mg/l, and there was no detectable nitrate at all. The water in our aquaria contains much more in the way of nitrogenous compounds. I tested for the levels of nitrogen in an 80 litre (about 15 gal.) tank filled with tap water and occupied by guppys. With normal feeding on *Tubifex* and *Daphnia*, the amount of total ammonia rose to 6.25 mg/l over 6 months and that of nitrate to 28.45 mg/l over the same period. These figures can rise even higher and then become harmful for the cryptocorynes as well as fish within the tank.

In order to grow cryptocorynes in the aquarium the structure of the substrate of the bed must be very important. The cryptocorynes in Johore grow in a light yellow, well bonded, gravelly-loam bed. The plants particularly *Cryptocoryne nurii*, were anchored by thick, white rhizomes. Digging up the plants out of this fine, sharp sand was a strenuous job that caused painful little nicks in the skin, particularly under the nails. Only rarely did we find this variety of cryptocoryne in a soft muddy, sandy loam. In Johore I never found cryptocoryne growing on boggy ground. The iron content in the soil substrate is, I think, very important. For growing cryptocoryne in the aquarium it is sensible to use a gravel fertiliser that contains adequate amounts of iron and all the other necessary trace elements for plant growth.

A characteristic feature of the natural habitat of cryptocorynes was that the localities were always well-shaded by vegetation overhanging from the bank and therefore the intensity of this shading was determined by the width of the water course.

The light intensity in the shade was exceptionally low and photographs could not be taken there without a flash. The light meter in my camera only showed ⅛ second, with the shutter at f. 2.8. In clearings where the sun managed to shine through the tree branches, the light values near the clumps of cryptocorynes were around 1000 Lux. We must take into account the fact that part of the light intensity is absorbed by the brownish water. So the cryptocorynes only receive a proportion of the light rays that reach the surface of the water, depending on the depth at which they are growing. I did not find cryptocorynes growing out of the water at any of the localities in Johore. *Cryptocoryne nurii* and *C. schulzei* are most definitely shade loving plants. Where the light is more intense physiological disorders arise in the plants, manifesting themselves as enzymatic changes in the plant cell nuclei. The assimilation activity is disturbed, the leaves die back and the whole plant perishes. Unsuitable light conditions are likely to be one of the reasons why the above-mentioned types of cryptocorynes grow so poorly in our tank.

The final essential factor is, I am convinced, temperature. In the rain forest, the streams I studied showed water tempera-

*Natural habitat of Cryptocoryne cordata.*

*Brachygobius (bumblebee fish) is occasionally found at the mouth of rivers.*

tures of 24° C (75° F). With air temperature of 30° C (90° F) during the day and with the relative humidity at 95–100%, the water in the forest streams seemed pleasantly cool. These values were measures in May, but in Malaysia the warm, humid, climate holds throughout the year. So the cryptocorynes from Johore have quite specific temperature requirements.
In the temperature in the aquarium is too low or too high, the growth of the plants may be inhibited and their susceptibility to disease increased.

Our second field trip took us south of Jemaluang in the direction of Kota Tinggi. For the most part this is a region of swampy rain forest and *Cryptocoryne cordata* grew in a large number of the forest streams that crossed our track. Here, in the typical habitat of *C. cordata*, I sought the solution to the problem of nomenclature in this species of cryptocoryne. Many different cryptocorynes are given the name of *C. cordata* by aquarists but it is not clear whether this species is really the one in question. It is interesting to note that in 1909 in the German magazine *Gartenwelt*, Baum had described the colour of the collar around the flower as bright yellow. Wendt also, in another publication wrote that the first imports (in 1906) had a collar that was either completely or mostly yellow. He took the view that, like many mountain plants culitvated in the lowlands, a change occurs in the colour of the collar. This colour modification, brought about by changes in temperature and light colour change in *C. cordata* had not been observed since 1925/26. In his opinion the colour of the collar in *C. cordata* is dark or blackish purple. Engler, de Wit and all authors of water plant treatises over the last few years have also described it as this colour. I went into this problem of nomenclature in the Herbarium of the University of Singapore. I found 17 different records of *C. cordata*, and in all the notes it stated "Fl. yellow" – i.e. yellow flowering. In 1978 Nils Jacobsen visited the localities where *C. cordata* is found in Johore. On his return he wrote to me that he could not find any difference between the type material of *C. cordata* and the yellow flowering variety of cryptocoryne from Johore. In one of his splendid publications he gave the colour of the collar as yellow.

*Cryptocoryne nurii with flower stalk and fruit.* ▷

I saw many *C. cordata* in the streams of the rain forest between Jemaluang and Kota Tinggi and many of them had just flowered. The colour of the tubular collar, which is not warty as in *C. purpurea* or *C. griffithii*, was always bright yellow. Not in a single case did I find the yellow colour merging to a brownish tone, not even at the edge of the tube. At various localities, *C. cordata* grows entirely submerged under the water. I did not see a single plant growing out of the water – even though the weather was dry and sunny in eastern Johore after the northeast monsoon. The plants were flowering in shallow water, and also at depths of 30–37.5 cm (12–15 inches). The length of the tube appeared to depend on the depth of the water. But the inflorescence (i.e. the flower on the cryptocoryne plant) always rose an inch (2,5 cm) or so, above the water surface and therefore it is difficult to quote the tube length as a taxonomic feature for purposes of description.

After thorough research in the native habitat of *C. cordata* I came to the conclusion

that this species has a bright yellow spathe collar and not a dark purple one as has been incorectly stated until now.

The numerous water courses in eastern Johore provide a home for many species of fish that are often kept in our aquaria. I was interested primarily in water plants, and it was my friend, Otto Hofmann, who was interested in the fish. His method of catching them was quite simple. Using a wide-necked hand net on a short handle, he made sweeps trough the plant-congested zone near the bank. Alternatively he fixed the hand net securely in position and waded through the plants, driving the fish before him into the net.

In the very first stream that crossed our road south of Mersing, he had a tremendous catch. It consisted mainly of *Dermogenis pusillus* (the half beak) which always lies in wait for its prey just below the surface of the water in their natural habitat these fish are beautifully coloured, to an extent that is never seen in an aquarium. There were also various rasboras. The most frequent and widely distributed

47

representative of this genus in Johore was *Rasbora heteromorpha* (harlequin fish). It was, in fact, brought to Europe for the first time in 1906 from the Botanical Gardens in Singapore, but Johore is the area where is widely distributed. Unfortunately, they are no longer to be found in the water courses of Singapore and the stocks of these fish in Johore has been severely decimated by irresponsible mass catching for export. Without doubt, the most beautiful species of rasbora are *Rasbora kalochroma* (iridescent rasbora) and *R. pauciperforata* (redlined rasbora) which we did not manage to cath in our shallow sweeps through the streams. We only had *Rasbora taeniata* in our net. Labyrinth fish were also very widespread in this area. In almost every stream we caught *Betta splendens* (Siamese fighting fish). *Trichopsis vittatus* (sparkling gourami) or *Trichogaster trichopterus* (three-spot gourami). *Sphaerichthys osphromenoides* (chocolate gou-

rami) were rather less common-much to my colleagues' displeasure.

On continuing our trip up to Kota Tinggi we stopped at many localities where *Cryptocoryne cordata* grew. Together with the usual labyrinth fish, *Dermogenus pusillus* and *Rasbora heteromorpha*, my friend's net often contained species of *Barbus*. The most frequent was *Barbus pentazona* (five banded barb) and *B. binotatus; B. everetti* (clown barb) and *B. lateristriga* (spanner barb) were the least common. We caught *Brachygobius nunus* (bumblebee fish) sporadically in river estuaries and in fresh water. The brackish water of the swampy lowland rain forest with its mangroves in the home of *Toxotes jaculator* (archer fish), *Aplocheilus panchax* and the mudskipper *Periophthalmus barbatus*. This brief summary shows just how rich the variety of plant and fish in East Johore is – I hope to return some day soon!

*Cryptocoryne affinis*

## Cryptocorynes in the aquarium

### Cryptocoryne affinis
*Native Habitat:*
Malayan Peninsula
This variety has been most popular during the last decade. On the upper side of the leaves, *C. affinis* shows a shining dark green-bluish dye, the under side a reddish-pale green color. With its lanceolate leaves that broaden towards the top, a striking effect is obtained due to the coloring of the foliage. This variety is of medium growth although the leaves may reach a length of 15 cm (6 inches); generally, however, they remain smaller.

The shape and the color of this plant depend mostly on external conditions: to a great extent on the light. *C. affinis* grows well in dim fluorescent light and only under this illumination reaches the best growth. The aquarist should bear this in mind when cultivating *C. affinis* and take it into account when planting this species. This variety can be very sensitive to a sudden increase in light intensity: the reaction may be a total decomposition of the leaves, which may be often interpreted as "cryptocoryne illness".

Apart from the above mentioned, *C. affinis* is one of the most rapidly growing species; it produces plenty of runners. With only few plants at the start the aquarist is in a position to obtain a fine stock within a short period of time. This variety accommodates very easily and should be used in the middle or the back according to the size of the tank. The dark foliage contrasts beautifully when planted in front of a group of plant showing pale green foliage.

### Cryptocoryne balansae
*Native Habitat:*
Thailand, Indochina
This species, with its very slender, deeply crinkled leaves, which may reach 30 cm (12 inches) and even more in length, does not represent the standard type of a *Cryptocoryne*. In fact, most of the *Cryptocoryne* varieties show more or less lanceolate or heart-shaped oval leaves and therefore it is often difficult to distinguish them because of their very similar form of the leaves and overall shapes of the plants.

*C. balansae* and a few other varieties are an exception from this rule. Due to the size of this plant (up to 50 cm [20 inches]), it is suited for lager tanks only. When planted in groups *C. balansae* adds a very decorative accent to the tank due to the unique structure of the leaves. With regard to cultivation *C. balansae* is rather accommodating with regard to light, on the other hand it is not very productive in the building of runners. Use of a fertiliser in preparing the gravel as well as the regular fertilization each change of water have a growth-promoting effect on this very species.

**Cryptocoryne cordata**
*Native Habitat:*
Thailand
This variety distinguishes itself by its leaves which are heart-shaped, oval, and rather

*Cryptocoryne cordata*

sturdy. It is very popular among aquarists because of its growth rate and its richness in color. The leaves are marked purple and ruby underneath and dark to light green with a reddish shade above. The size of the leaves varies from 5–10 cm (2–4 inches) and more. Growth and coloring depend to a certain degree on the placement in the tank; it is quite possible that the daily period of illumination is a factor as well. Different varieties of this species are known among aquarists: one with slim-shaped leaves, the other one with broader leaves. Just like *C. affinis*, this specimen is a "shadow" plant since it requires no direct light. After a short period of accommodation, a somewhat fertile substratum and the shading of some larger plants such as *Ceratopteris conuta*, it will grow rapidly. *C. cordata* is a variety which can be used in many ways for many purposes.

**Cryptocoryne ciliata**
*Native Habitat:*
From India to New Guinea
*C. ciliata* is an exceptional species, partly because of its large area of distribution. Its longish, lanceolate leaves may reach a length of 50 cm (20 inches). However, they do not grow that tall when submerged in an aquarium. Apart from smaller, narrow-leaved species which are commonly available, there are varieties from specific geographical regions. This superb specimen is ideal for every medium to large tank. Whether grouped in the middle or in the back, the shining pale-green stout leaves will attract the attention. Of course, adding fertiliser regularly to the gravel increases the rapid growth rate of this variety. Contrary to all other cryptocorynes, this species requires full illumination. Due to the size of this variety, shading by other plants will not take place. It is recommended not to reduce the period of illumination if *C. ciliata* is to become a superb beauty.

*Cryptocoryne ciliata*

In shallow tanks this variety grows beyond the surface of the water; it is therefore very well-suited for aquaterraria. This specimen belongs to the most easy-flowering varieties of cryptocorynes. Apart from runners, *C. ciliata* reproduces by shoots borne in a sheaf of leaves.

## Cryptocoryne willisii
*Native Habitat:*
Sri Lanka
The formerly "nevillii" is an unmistakable small, light green foreground plant. After a short period of acclimation, it produces numerous runners so that a splendid "lawn" may be obtained if the conditions in the tank are balanced. *C. willisii* is extremely accommodating and grows rapidly. Even repeated replanting is tolerated well while other *Cryptocoryne* species react with interruptions in their growth rate. Unlike other green cryptoco-

*Cryptocoryne willisii*

ryne, *C. willisii* needs as much light as possible. When planting, the aquarist has to make sure that it is not shaded by leaves of larger background plants. Apart from this *C. willisii* is very hardy and very long-lived, flourishing in either hard or soft water. Species of somewhat similar appearance include, *C. lucens* and *C. parva*. However, it is difficult for the aquarist to tell one from another.

## Cryptocoryne purpurea
*Native Habitat:*
Malaya
Plants offered under the name of *C. purpurea* are on occasion *C. griffithi*. In general, all cryptocorynes with more or less heart-shaped, dark green leaves are given this designation, or, to be exact, they are called "purpurea type". This is a practical solution as it is impossible for the hobbyist to differentiate among this group of cryptocorynes. Only when flowering (which happens very seldom in an aquarium) is a distinguishing feature given to the aquarist. *Cryptocoryne purpurea* are of medium and larger size, with heart-shaped, oval leaves, which are not longer than approximately 5–8 cm (2–3½ inches), borne on very long stalks. As far as cultivation, this species is not different from the general type of cryptocorynes. Accordingly, it thrives in dim light, requires the addition of tank fertilisers to the bottom gravel and a regular water change. It must be emphasized that peat filtration and *Blackwater Extract* also have a very favorable result.

## Cryptocoryne usteriana
*Native Habitat:*
Philippines
Just like *C. ciliata* this variety is one of the unusual types. It is regarded as one of the

*Cryptocoryne purpurea*

*Cryptocoryne usteriana*

most beautiful aquatic plants. Not only its impressive size, 80 cm (30 inches) but most of all the fantastically beautiful, hammered shining bright green structure of the leaves make this plant a jewel for every aquarium. Accordingly, the aquarist should give it a privileged place as a single plant, paying attention to the fact that it is only in tanks of a proper size this plant shows its best appearance. At the same time, sufficient illumination must be guaranteed so that *Cryptocoryne usteriana* may develop to full size.

*Cryptocoryne wendtii*

### Cryptocoryne wendtii
*Native Habitat:*
Sri Lanka
This is one of the most popular aquatic plants; is of medium height with leaves which are more or less lanceolate, broad at the base, sometimes heart-shaped and approximately 8–12 cm (3–5 inches) long. The upper surface is dark olive green; underneath this plant shows pale green to pale red colors. There are many variations of *Cryptocoryne wendtii*, different with regard to the size, form of the leaves, and coloration. Only when flowering is a distinguishing feature given to the aquarist. Perhaps the following facts may prove helpful to the hobbyist: within the entire family of cryptocorynes there exists no other species, growing more rapidly than *Cryptocoryne wendtii* and it cannot be surpassed by others with regard to accommodation and its growth rate, especially the production of runners. Extraordinary productivity makes this species, as well as *C. affinis* and *C. willisii*, especially suited for the beginning aquarist.

# Amazon Swordplants

In designing a geographically matched aquarium environment, the species of *Echinodorus* are "naturally" suited for South American tetras and non-digging South American cichlids and catfish. They are full plants forming centerpieces for naturally aquascaped aquariums. Compared to cryptocorynes, swordplants are very different in appearance. The most popular is the Amazon swordplant. However, a broad variety of *Echinodorus* are available, ranging from the small, grass-leaved *Echinodorus tenellus* to the giant species such as the large-leaved Amazon. New species are introduced regularly including the decorative *Echinodorus osiris*. Large plants, such as *Echinodorus bleheri* should be used as specimen plants while others which produce a less bold foliage should be planted as groups. Of course, this depends on the size of the aquarium.

Reproduction through runners takes place only in a few species, such as *E. tenellus* and *E. latifolius*. After a period of accommodation the large, stout species grows a bloom-stalk if the surroundings are favorable including full-spectrum daily illumination. This bloomstalk develops single, shrunken flowers, from which tiny new plants develop ... so-called adventitious plants. They grow stronger and stronger as they continue to reproduce. By weighting down the bloomstalk towards the tank bottom, these new plants will grow roots much more rapidly so that they may be detached from their parents after growing strong enough. These adventitious plants should be planted in a light part of the tank; shading by larger plants must be avoided.

Some *Echinodorus* species reach giant sizes after a reasonable period of time. It may take one to two years or even more until their development is finished and they become bold specimen plants.

The development of shrunken flowers indicates already that most *Echinodorus* species cannot be properly cultivated in an aquarium. In their native habitat they are marsh plants; while they can grow sufficiently submerged, they thrive partly submerged. A certain accommodation can be derived from the fact that many *Echinodorus* species have the tendency to produce aerial leaves. There is another fact which may indicate the character of their native habitat: as marsh plants they depend on genuine root nourishment. This means that the bottom material for a rapidly growing *Echinodorus* species should be fertilised, and fertiliser added at every water change. To obtain a true Amazon environment, regular use of *Spawning Aid* is most beneficial. Regular partial changes of water however are also important.

The following descriptions consider only the most prominent species. Other species which resemble the "swordplant type" have the same environmental requirements. Please bear in mind that most oft the "large" *Echimodorus* species become very large. When buying a small specimen as a young plant, its placement should be calculated in order to avoid having a plant that keeps growing and no longer fits in the preplanned aquascape.

**Echinodorus amazonicus**
*Native Habitat:*
Tropical South America
A desired aquatic plant for decades, known under different scientific names. Aquarists commonly called it "slender leaved Amazon". Its lanceolate, bright green leaves together with the stalk reach a length of more than 40 cm (15 inches); it remains a little bit smaller than *Echinodorus bleheri*. In aquascaping, *E. amazonicus* may be used in many ways and for many purposes. In a 190 l (50 gallon) tank, a middle group,

planted tight together, is very impressive. As a finishing plant in the back *E. amazonicus* looks very nice, also; in smaller tanks it should be planted alone. This species must be given ample space; only when the illumination intensity is strong enough does a single plant develop luxuriant growth.

**Echinodorus berteroi**
*Native Habitat:*
Central America and Neighboring Regions
This species is a completely different kind of *Echinodorus*. Its variable growth forms

*Echinodorus amazonicus*

*Echinodorus berteroi*

are striking. We distinguish a juvenile form with more or less linear, lanceolate leaves that may reach a length of 20 cm (8 inches). The leaves of the grown-up form broaden gradually and are slightly waved. Finally, the form of the leaf resembles that of the heart-shaped *Echinodorus cordifolis* but differs in view of the beautiful thin skinned structure of the olive-grenn leaves.

This plant species should not be planted in small tanks as its minimum height reaches almost 50 cm (16 inches). It has the tendency to grow over the water surface in order to build aerial leaves. Daily period of illumination to 12 hours is recommended.

Sometimes very stout plants will grow small side plants at the crown. Apart from this *E. berteroi* does not reproduce well in a tank. Flowering and germination can be obtained by longer light conditions. The sowing is not difficult; generally, however, the aquarist depends on the purchase of young plants. This plant belongs to the most decorative and characteristic varieties due to its transparency.

### Echinodorus cordifolius
*Native Habitat:*
Southeast North America to Mexico
Compared with other large swordplants, this plant has only the stout growth form in common. *Echinodorus cordifolius* deviates considerably with regard to the form of its leaves. At the base they are heart-shaped, becoming obtuse towards the top. In a favorable environment they may reach a length of 20 cm (8 inches) and a breadth of 15–21 cm (6½–8 inches). With its bright, shining green leaves and its striking, strong stalks, this species is especially suited as a single plant for large tanks. Grouping has no effect and is best not done in view of the size of this plant. It is important that *Echinodorus cordifolius* be cultivated in a tank with as high a water level as possible (approximately 60 cm [24 inches]). The young plants require intense illumination in order to develop into a stately specimen. In small tanks *Echinodorus cordifolius* grows very rapidly out of the water, a tendency it also has in large tanks. This may, however, be avoided by cutting down the period of illumination to 8–10 hours daily. By doing this, however, all other plants are interrupted in their growth rate as well. In case the aquarist wants to cultivate baby plants, which develop from the shrivelling bloom stalks of *Echinodorus cordifolius*, and to induce a strong growth rate in them, the period of illumination has to be extended (up to 16 hours). To induce *Echinodorus cordifolius* to flower (produce adventi-

*Echinodorus cordifolius*

tious plants), it is best to increase the period of lighting and to lower the water surface. This species will flower most successfully under very intense illumination. *Echinodorus cordifolius* is a very decorative center of attraction.

## Echinodorus bleheri
*Native Habitat:*
Tropical South America
Apart from the "slender-leaved Amazon", *Echinodorus bleheri* is one of the most cultivated and desirable aquatic plants. Its appearance resembles *Echinodorus amazonicus*, apart from the fact that it grows to a larger size. Its leaves may reach 40 cm (16 inches) in length and 8 cm (3 inches) in

width. In total this plant may, under favorable conditions, reach the size of 60 cm (24 inches). At this stage, *Echinodorus bleheri* develops an enormous quantity of leaves; accordingly, it is recommended to cultivate this plant only if at least a 114 l (30 gallon) tank is available to the hobbyist, as only in large-sized tanks does this plant shows its real beauty. If this Amazon plant is allowed to grow in the right surroundings, it will become the dominating factor in a tank, thereby lessening the living conditions for all other plants in the same aquarium. When choosing a place for *Echinodorus bleheri*, the aquarist should take into account its larger size, as the shading does not allow other plants to grow. Even plants that are extremely accommodating in respect to light will not grow. As most varieties of *Echinodorus*, *Echinodorus bleheri* requires continual full-spectrum lighting. According to recent investigations, variable leaf forms which have often been observed, depend obviously on the period of illumination. Consequently the hobbyist can be assured that it is not a question of different species. Compared with the small "slender-leaved Amazon", *Echinodorus bleheri* does not produce bloom stalks very often, so that reproduction activities are not very common. A stout plant like *Echinodorus bleheri* should of course be given a fertile substratum with a depth of at least 8–10 cm (3–4 inches).

*Echinodorus bleheri*

### Echinodorus latifolius

(Often named *E. magdalenensis,* sometimes called *E. grisebachii*)

*Native Habitat:*

Columbia and neighboring regions. *Echinodorus latifolius* is an Amazon swordplant of medium size, building numerous runners and producing bushes of gold foliage under proper conditions. This plant is eminently suitable as as centerpiece or as a striking foreground plant in larger tanks. If maintained alone, this plant loses most of its attractiveness. The larger and thicker the shining green foliage, the more beautiful *Echinodorus latifolius* looks. With regard to the structure of the leaves, it has variable growth forms, which depend on the intensity of illumination, the daily length of lighting, and the temperature.

The leaves reach a maximum length of 15 cm (6 inches); in most cases, however, they remain considerably smaller. They are of a bright green color, lanceolate, and show a distinct middle vein. *Echinodorus latifolius* has proven itself to be a species which is extremely accommodating and most easily acclimated. Your dealer may offer this plant sometimes as *Echinodorus intermedius,* a name which is used for *Echinodorus quadricostatus* as well. Both varieties have a certain resemblance. *Echinodorus quadricostatus,* however, remains smaller wuth somewhat broader leaves. Due to the conditions of light and placement, these differences may not become apparent. Accordingly, confusion between species arises frequently.

*Echinodorus latifolius*

## Echinodorus maior

*Native Habitat:*

Tropical South America

*Echinodorus maior* can easily be distinguished from the other species of the genus. The relatively short, round leaf stem, which is flattened on one side, rises out of a strong cylindrical root stock. The base of the leaf is usually rounded and the tip cut off short. Of the 5 to 7 primary veins which appear on the lower side, at least two originate in the central rib and end with the latter at the tip. The others rise from the base of the leaf and run out at the edge, which is strikingly wavy and sometimes even folded. The fully-grown yellowish-lush green leaf reaches an average length of 67.5 cm (27 inches) and a width of up to 12.5 cm (5 inches). Because swordplants have roots which run along the upper layers of the ground, the gravel does not need to be deeper than 10 cm (4 inches).

With regard to the hardness and salt content of the water *Echinodorus maior* is fairly adaptable. Only a lack of iron in the water results in deficiency symptoms. It does not require any special lighting.

*Echinodorus maior* is ideal as the focal point or eye-catcher in large tanks.

## Echinodorus parviflorus

*Native Habitat:*

Tropical South America

This medium-sized species is mostly known under the trade name of *Echinodorus peruensis*. Its lanceolate leaves that turn dark green during their development frequently broaden towards the base and may attain a length of 20–25 cm (8–10 inches) when measure together with the stalk. Obtuse leaf forms appear when the light period is reduced. The temperature range

*Echinodorus maior*

*Echinodorus parviflorus*

of *Echinodorus parviflorus* is rather broad; also with its light requirements this plant is very accommodating. *Echinodorus parviflorus* is a handsome group plant for larger tanks.

## Echinodorus tenellus

*Native Habitat:*
From Tropical America to North America
The pygmy chain Amazon shares only the generic name with other Amazon plants since it resembles *Sagittaria*. *Echinodorus tenellus* is very common in America and its tropical variety is cultivated in tanks. *Echinodorus tenellus* is one of the most durable aquatic plants. With its extremely delicate, elongated, grasslike leaves which only become 5 cm (2 inches) in length, it produces within a very short time a thick, light green "carpet" due to extremely frequent building of runners. *Echinodorus tenellus* is one of the most popular aquatic plants, extremely suited as a foreground plant. The aquarist, however, cultivating the pygmy chain Amazon has to pay attention to the fact that this species needs full light if he wants to obtain a compact, healthy, thick carpet. Since light decreases significantly when measured from the top to the bottom of the tank, especially in large tanks, this fact must be considered when planting new plants and when installing new light fittings.

Another new plant not pictured but highly recommended is *Echinodorus osiris*, a stout, genuine sword plant, similar to *E. bleheri*. The leaves of *Echinodorus osiris*, however, are distinctly broader in the upper part; the juvenile form has a very decorative reddish dye.

*Echinodorus tenellus*

61

With respect to the proper scientific names of the *Echinodorus* genus, below please find a summary of the socalled "Amazon swordplants":

1. Name: Pygmy Chain Amazon
   Valid scientific name: *Echinodorus tenellus*

2. Name: Little (Small) Amazon
   Valid scientific name: *Echinodorus quadricostatus*
   Formerly: *Echinodorus intermedius*

3. Name: Pygmy Amazon
   Valid scientific name: *Echinodorus latifolius*
   Formerly: *E. magdalenensis, E. intermedius*

4. Name: Black Amazon
   Valid scientific name: *Echinodorus parviflorus*
   Formerly: *Echinodorus peruensis*

5. Name: Ruffled Amazon
   Valid scientific name: *Echinodorus maior*
   Formerly: *E. martii, E. leopoldina*

6. Name: Slender-Leaved Amazon
   Valid scientific name: *Echinodorus amazonicus*
   Formerly: *E. brevipedicellatus*

7. Name: *Large Amazon* or *Large-Leaved Amazon*
   Valid scientific name: *Echinodorus bleheri*
   Formerly: *E. paniculatus*

8. Name: Red Amazon
   Valid scientific name: *Echinodorus osiris*
   Formerly: *E. rübra*

# SOME SPECIAL AQUARIUM PLANTS

If all aquatic plants could thrive under exactly the same tank conditions, the aquarist would hardly experience any difficulties or challenges in maintaining a successful natural planted aquarium.

In absolute terms however, every aquatic plant has its own specific requirements with respect to light, water conditions, and planting conditions. Nevertheless, there is something like a set of "standard conditions" to which most aquatic plants accommodate themselves. This accommodation allows the combining of different species to form "unnatural" communities. Plants may even thrive despite the "unnatural" setting if the important guidelines reviewed elsewhere in this book are followed.

There are, however, "outsiders", which cannot acclimate to the created uniformity in an aquarium due to their specific native habitats. Most of these come from regions with climates of extreme seasonal changes, to which these plants are accustomed. They are so conditioned to these seasonal adaptations that they follow their lifecycle even if not forced by the external conditions of aquarium life. These plants undergo dormant lifeless periods and then suddenly bloom or grow magnificently. The aquarist can do nothing to change this phenomenon.

Typical representatives of such individualistic aquatic plants are called *Aponogeton*. When planting a bulb which has been im-

ported during the rest period, the aquarist may enjoy the rapid, gorgeous growth of this plant for several months. All *Aponogeton* species have a remarkable growth rate; leaf after leaf develops and finally the formation of flowers takes place. After that, however, the vitality of the plant decreases and the rest period starts. Importantly, during cultivation in an aquarium, this rest has to be granted, if the hobbyist wants to enjoy this peculiar, beautiful plant for a longer period of time. Actually, this is a "secret" to the successful cultivation of *Aponogeton*: by recognizing this dormancy the hobbyist will be able to enjoy the characteristic transparent and often very peculiar leaf structure of the truly unique *Aponogeton* aquatic plants (see below).

It is recommended to plant the bulbs immediately into a small pot; this makes an easy removal from the tank when the rest period starts. When buying *Aponogeton* bulbs during the rest period (i.e. without leaves) the aquarist does not know for sure which varietes will develop, and this will make the cultivation even more exciting.

Other aquatic plants reviewed in this section have special requirements differing from all the above-mentioned plants. Some examples are: the beautiful *Barclaya*, belonging to the family of the water lilies; the delicate *Blyxa* species and finally a garden plant which has been changed into an aquatic plant, *Saururus*.

## Aponogeton boivinianus

*Native Habitat:*

Madagascar

Recently this very decorative species has become more available, although not always under its correct name. The aquarist, however, often has a clue to *Aponogeton boivinianus* the bulbs are rather stout, having a diameter of approximately 4 cm (1½ inches). And at the same time are flat and grooved. If the bulb has sprouted and shows the typical, strongly grooved leaf, which resembles *Cryptocoryne usteriana*, this is an unmistakable characteristic immediately identifying *Aponogeton boivinianus*.

There is one point which the aquarist has to recognize immediately. *Aponogeton boivinianus* grows very rapidly! Its wrinkled leaves attain a length of 50 cm (20 inches) and more, which makes this species unsuit-ed for smaller tanks. It is, however, one of the most beautiful of all aquatic plants, with no other special requirement.

## Aponogeton crispus

*Native Habitat:*

Sri Lanka, Ceylon

Compared to *Aponogeton boivinianus*, the rootstock of this species is somewhat rounder and much smaller. The oblong, lanceolate (approximately 30 cm [12 inches]) long leaves, show the typical crinkled margin. Frequently hybrids grow larger than the genuine *Aponogeton crispus*. It is, however, not certain if the genuine species now offered as an aquatic plant is pure-bred. It is possible that

*Aponogeton boivinianus*

*Aponogeton crispus*

breedings with *Aponogeton undulatus* have produced many hybrids. Regardless, this species is the most popular to be cultivated in aquariums. Its cultivation is highly recommended as it poses no problems. *Aponogeton crispus* will not thrive if the aquarist skips one rest period (i.e. if he does not take this plant out of the tank after growth has stopped and keeps it in a cool place).

If this plant is left in a tank it forms a new bloomstalk after a short period of time. In the long run this is not recommended, since even the most hardy plant cannot stand this exhausting treatment over the course of time.

### Aponogeton madagascariensis
*Nuilve Habitat:*
Madagascar
The Madagascar lace plant is the most popular and desirable plants of this family

*Aponogeton madagascariensis*

due to the peculiar and unique structure of its leaves. At the same time, it offers the most problems.

Obviously there exist different geograhical varieties; plants with rather broad, rounded leves and plants with leaves that are more slender and pointed. The biology of the characteristic leaf structure – in the course of the leaves' development only the vein structure remains in the end – is mysterious. It is frequently assumed that the perforated surface of the leaves reduces the flow resistance of the leaves. Contrary to this assumption, however, *Aponogeton madagascariensis* is found in still waters and flowing waters.

Plants of the slender-leaved type thrive best in semi-shaded tanks or when exposed to full illumination at a distance from the tank bottom to the light reflector of 40 cm (16 inches). More important, however, is the regular adding of fresh water to which peat extracts (*Spawning Aid*) have been added and continuous peat filtration.

Cultivation of this plant is only possible when changing at least ⅔ of the tank volume weekly. The water hardness should be less than 10° dH; the water temperature should be kept at 70° F (or 22° C). When a rest period occurs, the water temperature should be lowered to 66° F or 18° C – at night to 60° F or 15° C for a period of 2 months. After this time a new growth period will take place. Under these conditions, *Aponogeton madagascariensis* may be kept for many years. However, these conditions cannot be maintained in a normal show tank, so that this plant should be kept only by the very dedicated hobbyist who will appreciate its "starring role" in a tropical aquarium.

The non-dedicated hobbyist should refrain from purchasing these delicate species, especially in view of the fact that mass imports may endanger the wild reserves.

## Aponogeton ulvaceus
*Native Habitat:*
Madagascar

With its very large, undulating, bright green leaves which may attain a length of 50 cm (20 inches), *Aponogeton ulvaceus* is one of the most attractive single plants in an aquarium. Its rapid growth rate enables the aquarist within a few months to realize a giant plant from a young specimen. This species requires an enriched substrate, as well as an unimpeded light source in order to become a really gorgeous plant! Most of all, *Aponogeton ulvaceus* should be given ample space so that is may develop its size and full beauty. For months *A. ulvaceus* will be the center of attraction in any aquarium.

*Aponogeton ulvaceus* produces many bloomstalks with two spikes (a successful fertilization, however, can only occur if another plant is flowering at the same time). The beginning of the rest period can be easily observed when growth is reduced. The leaves remain smaller and narrower. At this point the hobbyist should remove *Aponogeton ulvaceus* from the tank and plant it into a flower pot. The plant will overcome this transplanting without any risk to its life. The rootstock should be kept cool and wet; it is, however, not necessary to keep the rootstock submerged in water all the time. When the new growth period starts, the composition of the substrate should be renewed. The rootstock should not be planted too deeply (the top must be

*Aponogeton ulvaceus*

just above the surface of the gravel). This is true for all *Aponogeton* species.

## Aponogeton undulatus
*Native Habitat:*
From India to the Malayan Peninsula
This variable species remains relatively small most of the time, i.e. the undulating stalked leaves reach a length of only 25 cm (10 inches). The thick tube rootstock has a diameter of 2 cm (¾ inch). Its light to middlegreen colored leaves show peculiar, translucent zones. This is characteristic of this species and allows the aquarist to easily tell *Aponogeton undulatus* from other *Aponogeton* varieties.

*Aponogeton undulatus* may be used for many purposes; planted in small groups or as a single plant in small sized tanks. A trait which is characteristic to this plant and which saves the aquarist from the rather troublesome problem of reproduction is that *Aponogeton undulatus* produces presumptuous bloomstalks with tiny ready-built young plants with bulbs; in a certain way this plant can be called a "viviparous" specimen, enabling the aquarist to plant the baby plants immediately. A rest period in order to bring an old rhizome back to vitality is not needed with *Aponogeton undulatus*, as continually new plants are produced and they in turn grow rapidly. It is a very recommendable species which offers no cultivation problems.

## Barclaya longifolia
*Native Habitat:*
Burma, Thailand, Indochina
This aquatic plant is one of the most beautiful among the aquatic flora. Unfortunately, it is rather expensive when available.
According to current knowledge, the native habitat of *Barclaya longifolia* is in shaded jungle streams, similar to several *Cryptocoryne* species. It is, however, much more delicate and demanding than *Cryptocoryne*, *Barclaya* likes water temperatures of 75° F–82° F (24 to 30° C), the substratum must be enriched. It is important that the gravel has the same temperature as the water as most failures can be immediately traced to too low bottom temperatures. A difference of only 2 degrees is enough to cause distrubances in the growth rate. Therefore a downward flow of water-adjacent to the heater or a sub-gravel heater is recommended. *Barclaya longifolia* has special lighting requirements. If the oblong, slender, undulating leaves with

*Aponogeton undulatus*

*Barclaya longifolia*

**Blyxa** (various species)
*Native Habitat:*
Eastern Asia

As "*Blyxa japonica*" or only under the name of "*Blyxa*", several varieties of this species from tropical Southeast Asia are offered for sale. They are genuine water plants. They have a characteristic shape recognizable in view of their somewhat translucent, light green to brownish-green, grasslike often fragile leaves. In an aquarium they are of high decorative value, especially when planted in the center. According to our experiences all *Blyxa* varieties need so much light that they cannot be maintained in an aquarium for long periods. These species, apart from few exceptions, never make good aquarium plants. Often they stop growing after a short period of time, become unsightly, and the aquarist has to replace them. In terms of water conditions, frequent partial water changes need to be made.

their beautifil reddish-olive-green coloration are to attain their full length (up to 50 cm [20 inches]), the hobbyist should expose the plant to full illumination. If this plant is kept in proper surroundings, it might develop a small decorative flower. The production of seed has been observed occasionally; reproduction, however, can more easily be done with the help of the rhizome shoots. These young plants should be cultivated in bright surroundings and at temperatures of 84° F (28° C) in shallow water. Water hardness up to 10° dH is suited and regular water change is necessary. *Barclaya* is a unique single plant for aquariums of medium size.

*Blyxa species*

## Nuphar luteum

*Native Habitat:*

Europe, Asia

*Nuphar luteum* is a plant for very large aquariums. The aquarist appreciates not only its "normal" floating leaves and flowers which he knows from indigenous water lilies, but also the shining, bright green, oval-formed or elongated under-water leaves that may attain a length of approximately 20 cm (8 inches) and more. *Nuphar luteum* has fleshy, but very delicate rootstocks. When buying this plant the aquarist should pay attention to the fact that these rootstocks do not show foul spots. In an aquarium this plant should be established using suitable fertilisers, with full illumination; the rootstock should be buried, but the upper part should be at, or just above, the surface of the gravel.

Although this plant comes from temperate regions it can be easily kept in tropical tanks. Under proper conditions it grows to a gorgeous single plant, adding uncomparable beauty to a tank. Because of the tendency to build floating leaves, a water depth of 80 cm (33 inches) is required.

*Nuphar luteum*

## Saururus cernuus

*Native Habitat:*

Northern America

As in the case of *Lobelia cardinalis*, this is a genuine land plant converted to life in a tropical tank. *Saururus cernuus* grows rapidly and has few special maintenance requirements. This highly decorative plant is recommended to any aquarist.

Established as a single plant in the foreground or grouped in larger quantities, *Saururus cernuus* is extremely accommodating and beautiful. The hobbyist, however, should pay attention to one fact: good light is necessary for the development of stout, compact plants. Otherwise *Saururus cernuus* grows tall, thin stalks instead of acting as a bottom plant.

*Saururus cernuus*

# Ferns and mosses in the aquarium

Fern and moss species – i.e. plants which do not belong to the *flowering* plants – have extremely different varieties suitable for aquariums. Often a splendid specimen of the Indian fern, *Ceratopteris thalictroides*, may reach such a size that this plant with its bright green, fine leaves becomes the dominating plant in a medium sized tank. On the other hand a delicate moss-like *Vesicularia dubyana* with its tiny leaves can be effectively developed as a graceful, fine group established in the branches of wooden roots or between rock groups. All species mentioned in this book, however, are extremely well-suited for tank life. They offer a variety of uses and have only few special requirements. Their best advantage is that they often add the "certain something" to an underwater landscape which is necessary for the completion of a true "underwater garden". If treated properly, ferns and moss turn out to be perennial plants.

**Ceratopteris thalictroides**
*Native Habitat:*
Tropical Regions of the world
The Indian fern is well-known among long-

*Ceratopteris thalictroides*

*Ceratopteris pteridoides*

time aquarists. This plant with its finely dissected fronds has been kept for decades in aquariums. Apart from full-spectrum light, it needs slightly acid but not too hard water. Peat extracts (*Spawning Aid*) and peat filtration are advisable.

*Ceratopteris thalictroides*, generally known as water spirte, is a beautiful Asiatic plant that has several uses in the aquarium. Water sprite has two distinct forms, depending upon whether it is floating or rooted. Another floating species is *Ceratopteris pterioides* from the warmer parts of America.

Water sprite is a very easy plant to maintain. Although it comes from acid waters with a pH between 5 and 6.5, it adapts nicely to somewhat alkaline conditions. It does require a temperature always above 68° F (20° C). Water sprite also does best when provided with strong lighting.

Propagating water sprite is simple. The leaves, particularly on the floating form, develop buds, which, in turn, grow into new plants. These buds can either be removed to grow on their own or left attached to the parent. If part of a leaf is broken off, which happens easily as they are fragile, the fragment will probably bud and become a new plant.

Water sprite is a fairly soft plant. A number of species of fish and most snails will dine on it, and although it reproduces rather rapidly, its succulence may soon cause it to disappear from an aquarium.

Water sprite provides several potential benefits to an aquarium. For example, a large cluster of the floating form serves as a good hiding place for baby fish or harassed adults. Also, a good surface cover filters the lighting and creates a favorable environment for some species of *Cryptocoryne*. The more timid types of fish derive a sense of security when the water surface is overgrown with floating plants. In short, there is probably a place in every aquarium for water sprite, a beautiful and useful plant.

## Riccia fluitans
*Native Habitat:*
All over the world
This is a floating group plant, meaning that the single delicate plants must be established as a mass. *Riccia fluitans* has been a popular and aproved aquatic plant for decades. If floats just beneath the surface of the water, surviving extremely well in spite of high temperatures. This plant grows so well that the aquarist has to "thin it out" frequently. As such, he is in a position to give this floating plant to other aquarists. The underwater sight of *Riccia fluitans* adds a special accent to the tank, a little bit more "jungle", as all floating plants do. *Riccia fluitans* is valued as a spawning plant and bubblenest-building fish also use it as footing for teir nests. To prevent *R. fluitans* from being overrun by algae and to ensure it a long life aquarium water must be changed regularly. *R. fluitans* is especially sensitive to the build-up of waste substances.

## Microsorium pteropus
*Native Habitat:*
Southeast Asia, tropical regions
*Microsorium pteropus* is a completely different kind of fern. Its bright to middle-green leaves which are undivided may attain a length of 30 cm (12 inches). They are more or less lanceolate and older leaves show rooted adventitious plants. This fern should never be used as a bottom plant as it then looks rather boring. *Microsorium pteropus* is more of a "branch plant", which should be anchored with the help of a fine plastic wire to a piece of driftwood. Here it develops roots and after a shourt period of time it thrives and starts growing. This fern is very decorative when used as a "dressing" for wooden roots. *M. pteropus* is very accomodating as regards light requirements, and still thrives with moderate illumination. Regular water change and peat filtration are further factors that lead to a healthy growth.

*Above: Riccia fluitans*
*Below: Microsorium pteropus*

## Vesicularia dubyana
*Native Habitat:*
Southeast Asia, especially Indonesia, Philippines
A very graceful, fine, delicate water moss, *Vesicularia dubyana* has bright green, very delicate leaves. It is rather frail in appear-

ance but can be very useful as a spawning plant. For decorative purposes it may be fastened to wooden roots where it will grow rather strongly. Fastened to decorative rocks it will slowly grow. With respect to illumination, *Vesicularia dubyana* turns out to be as accommodating as any other aquatic plant. But it will thrive better and more rapidly when exposed to full illumination. It is important that there are not bottom feeding fish species in the same tank as *Vesicularia dubyana*, as they stir up waste particles, lying on the tank bottom, which in turn are trapped in the moss bunches. Strong aeration should be avoided, too. Bunches that have become unsightly in the course of the time should be washed in a water-filled bucket. They should be then fastened to their former location. With regard to temperature. *Vesicularia dubyana* is very accommodating; it continues to grow even at temper-

atures under 68° F (20° C). The best temperature, however, seems to be 75°–82° F (24–28° C).

*Vesicularia dubyana*

# AQUATIC PLANTS – TROUBLE SHOOTING

Occasionally the hobbyist may find that his aquatic plants are no longer growing or have lost much of the attractiveness of their original appearance. The chances of this happening if the guidelines are followed as outlined in this book are slim but nevertheless the hobbyist should have available some idea of the causes and preventive measures when his plants are not prospering. The purpose of this section is to provide a check list for the most common plant defects and problems.

The most important rule is to determine the cause of the problem and to take proper *preventive measures*. If your plants are not prospering, you should immediately review the following points:

● have you prepared the base material with suitabe fertiliser?
● are you regularly fertilizing the water?
● are you using full spectrum lighting and changing the tubes as directed?
● are the hours of lighting consistent with the needs of the plants?
● are you paying strict attention to the temperature requirements of the plants; are the roots too cool?
● have you checked pH and hardness to make sure the water quality is correct?
● is the water being changed regularly? Plants, like fish, are intolerant of the buildup of nitrite and this can only be alleviated by a regular program of water changes and good filtration.
● are your maintenance practices consistent, that is, are you changing approximately 20% of the water every 10–14 days? Significant variations from established procedures can cause stress, not only to fish but to plants as well.

To protect both fish and plants in a alanced fresh water aquarium *Tetra AquaSafe* and *Spawning Aid* should be used regularly. *AquaSafe* helps plants absorb valuable trace elements from the water and protects the leaves and stems from injury. *Spawning Aid* creates a favorable peaty water environment and restricts the growth of algae. It is particularly valuable in "Amazon" aquariums containing discus, angels and neons. The following is a table to use as a check list for plant defects and growth rate interruptions.

| Appearance | Cause | Prevention |
|---|---|---|
| **A.** Although the plants grow they have thin stalks and a thin appearance (this can especially be observed with stalk plants). Leaves often show a pale-green color (see also B, C) | Lack of light or neglect of the different light requirements of different species (see description of species in the text). | Increase illumination, i.e. new fluorescent tubes should be installed. The number of tubes depends on the distance from water surface to bottom, and on the quality and strength of the bulb. (See lighting section). |
| **B.** Growth rate becomes erratic; reproduction occurs only in few cases or not at all. Damaged leaves can be observed. | | General rules: Immediately make partial water change. *AquaSafe* and *Spawning Aid* should be added to the fresh water, peat filtration should be added. |
| a) Standstill of the growth process without any visible damage | Water may be too alkaline, check the pH-value. | Water change, if the pH-value essentially exceeds 7.5 peat filtration as above. |
| b) Distortion in growth rate without any visible sign. From time to time leaves show hard cal careous deposits. | Carbon dioxide missing in the tank water; increase in the pH. | Leaves with calcareous deposits – as *Nomaphila* species – always indicate acute lack of carbon dioxide. Adding of fresh water should be increased, further lack of carbon dioxide by too intensive aeration should be avoided. Peat filtration, *AquaSafe* and *Spawning Aid* stabilize the pH-value. Consider adding more fish or removing plants. |
| c) Leaves (especially among plants of rapid growth) show a pale-green, partly yellowish-green coloration. Retardation of the growth rate. | Lack of nutritive substances especially iron. | Water change, *AquaSafe* and *Spawning Aid* should be added to the water, as well as regular additions of suitable fertilisers. |
| d) Signs of decay or tiny spots on the leaves. The symptoms of the so-called "Cryptocoryne-illness" belong to this category. | The tank water may be out of balance, often too high nitrogen content. Check nitrite, check-pH-value, too. Possibly the content of chlorides may be too high. | Tank water should be more frequently changed. Overcrowding of the tank should be avoided, perhaps the quantity of fish should be decreased. Be sure no salt is added to the tank water as it does harm to most aquatic plants. |

75

| Appearance | Cause | Prevention |
|---|---|---|
| e) Easily visible leaf damage (Amazon swordplants show brownish areas and leaves with brown margins). | Different causes, often lack of calium or poor aeration and foulness of gravel bed. | Check the pH-value and the structure of the bottom material (foul smelling bottom indicates lack of oxygen). Water change adding *Aqua Safe*. |
| **C.** The plants show distinctly visible damages but keep growing slowly. | | |
| a) Distinct roundish holes in the leaf surface. Most of the time only with delicate plants. | Most likely snails. | New plants should always be checked for snails and their spawn on the leaves. Leaves with spawn should be removed. Do not place in the tank. All new plants should be checked very carefully. |
| b) Plants, especially the delicate ones, look like they often have been torn up. | Certain aquarium fish are not only vegetarians but also prefer the delicate leaves of water plants. | It is recommended to use stout plants only particularly if the hobbyist keeps fish which show any tendency to eat plants. The fish diet should be supplemented with *Conditioning Food*. |
| c) Algae overtakes plants; older leaves show a thick algae carpet or the plants are covered with a filthy dark blue-green algae. | The pH-value should be checked. Often green algae thrive in water that is too "old", i.e. has not been changed frequently enough. A very low pH will confirm this. Under these conditions algae colonize the plant leaves, an unbalanced supply of nutritive substances (nitrogen, phosphate, see under B., d) may also be a reason. | For prevention, see B (general rule). Intensive peat filtration is necessary, as well as algae control in general. When setting up the aquarium for the first time see information at the start of this book. |

# SUMMARY CARE TABLE OF 50 POPULAR AQUATIC PLANTS

(in alphabetical order)

| Scientific Name/Origin | Specifications | | |
| --- | --- | --- | --- |
| | Light | Temperature | Comments |
| Acorus grammineus var. pusillus<br>Eastern Asia | high | 15–20°C<br>48–68°F | A very decorative foreground plant which is not perennial in warm water. If possible, do not place in high temperatures. |
| Aponogeton boivinianus<br>Madagascar | high | 22–28° C<br>70–80° F | A very decorative plant which makes an ideal single plant for large aquariums. Does best if rest period is strictly observed. |
| Aponogeton crispus<br>Sri Lanka | high | 20–28° C<br>68–80° F | Very enduring plant, easily cultivated without special requirements. Can be used as a single plant in medium size aquarium. |
| Aponogeton madagascariensis<br>Madagascar | high | about 22° C<br>70° F | Very popular due to its unique leaf structure but not easily cultivated. Frequent water changes are necessary; used primarily as a single plant. |
| Aponogeton ulvaceus<br>Madagascar | high | 22–28° C<br>70–80° F | Highly recommended as a single plant. To maximize beauty, rest period must be observed. |

|  |  | Specifications |  |
| --- | --- | --- | --- |
| **Scientific Name/Origin** | **Light** | **Temperature** | **Comments** |
| Aponogeton undulatus<br>India, Malayan Peninsula | moderate<br>to high | 20–28° C<br>70–80° F | Does best as a group plant in large and medium size aquariums. Only in smaller tanks should it be used as a single plant. Easily reproduces without special requirements. |
| Bacopa caroliniana<br>North America | high | 16–24° C<br>50–75° F | A slow growing plant requiring full light from above. Suitable only when planted in groups but does well in every size aquarium. |
| Barclaya longifolia<br>Burma, Thailand | high | 24–30° C<br>75–89° F | One of the most beautiful aquatic plants. A decorative showpiece which should be planted singly. Substrate must be kept warm and occasionally fertilised. |
| Blyxa species<br>Eastern Asia | very high | 22–28° C<br>70–80° F | This plant requires intense illumination. Should be planted as a group in the aquarium center. |
| Cabomba species<br>Tropical America | very high<br>to high | 20–28° C<br>68–80° F | One of the most beautiful stalk plants. Extremely decorative as a group planting. |
| Ceratopteris thalictroides<br>Worldwide, Tropical Regions | high | 22–26° C<br>70–78° F | Highly recommended and very enduring as long as it receives full light. Best used as a single plant in small and medium size aquariums. |
| Cryptocoryne affinis<br>Malayan Peninsula | moderate | 22–28° C<br>70–80° F | A rapid growing, highly decorative plant which makes a beautiful effect when planted in a group. |
| Cryptocoryne balansae<br>Thailand, Indochina | moderate<br>to high | 22–28° C<br>70–80° F | A relatively slow growing plant requiring a large aquarium. It is suitable both as a single plant and as a group plant. |

| Scientific Name/Origin | Specifications | | |
|---|---|---|---|
| | Light | Temperature | Comments |
| Cryptocoryne cordata<br>Thailand | moderate | 22–28° C<br>70–80° F | A rapid growing, highly decorative plant which does best in the "shadow" of larger plants. It's suited for a group plant for larger aquariums. |
| Cryptocoryne ciliata<br>Southeast Asia | high | 22–28° C<br>70–80° F | Very enduring and decorative as long as it receives full illumination. Makes an excellent single plant in smaller tanks and is better planted as a group in medium and large aquariums. |
| Cryptocoryne purpurea<br>Malayan Peninsula | moderate | 22–28° C<br>70–80° F | An enduring beautiful plant which should be planted as a group in larger aquariums. |
| Cryptocoryne willisii<br>(= C. "nevillii")<br>Sri Lanka | moderate to high | 22–28° C<br>70–80° F | A highly recommended rapid growing plant which should be positioned directly under the light; makes an excellent foreground plant for all aquarium sizes. |
| Cryptocoryne usteriana<br>Philippines | high | 22–28° C<br>70–80° F | Effective only as a single plant in very large aquariums; requires full illumination. |
| Cryptocoryne wendtii<br>Sri Lanka | moderate | 29–28° C<br>70–80° F | A highly recommended, rapidly growing decorative plant which should always be planted as a group. |
| Echinodorus amazonicus<br>Tropical South America | moderate | 24–28° C<br>75–80° F | A beautiful plant suitable as a group plant in large aquariums or as a single plant in medium and small aquariums. Highly recommended as it is a most accommodating species. |

| Scientific Name/Origin | Specifications | | |
| --- | --- | --- | --- |
| | Light | Temperature | Comments |
| Echinodorus berteroi<br>Central America | high | 20–26° C<br>68–80° F | Not always an enduring plant but appreciated for its large stalk. Should be planted as a single plant in large aquariums. |
| Echinodorus bleheri<br>Tropical South America | high | 24–28° C<br>75–80° F | Easily cultivated with rapid growth. Single plant with abundant leaf development. Suitable only for large aquariums. |
| Echinodorus cordifolius<br>Mexico | high | 20–26° C<br>68–80° F | Rapid growing and enduring. Looks best as a single plant in large aquariums. |
| Echinodorus latifolius<br>Tropical South America | high | 22–28° C<br>70–80° F | Easily cultivated. Produces abundant runners. Very attractive as a group plant. |
| Echinodorus maior<br>South America | high | 22–28° C<br>70–80° F | Highly recommendable and enduring as long as it receives full light from above. May be utilized as both a single plant and in groups. |
| Echinodorus parviflorus<br>South America | high | 22–28° C<br>70–80° F | Highly decorative. Makes a beautiful group planting in large aquariums. |
| Echinodorus tenellus<br>South to North America | high | 20–26° C<br>68–80° F | Highly recommended, beautiful foreground plant; should not be shaded. |
| Egeria densa<br>Argentina | high | 14–22° C<br>48–70° F | An enduring coldwater plant which should be planted in mid-tank in bunches. |
| Heteranthera zosterifolia<br>South America | high | around 24° C<br>75° F | Highly recommended as a group plant. Requires full light from above. |

| Scientific Name/Origin | Specifications | | |
|---|---|---|---|
| | **Light** | **Temperature** | **Comments** |
| Hydrocotyle leucocephala<br>South America | high | 22–25° C<br>70–80° F | Rapid growing, enduring plant. Best utilized in the foreground. |
| Hydrocotyle vulgaris<br>Europe | high | maximum<br>25° C<br>80° F | Suitable as a foreground plant in cold water aquariums. |
| Hygrophila difformis<br>India to Malayan Peninsula | high | 22–28° C<br>70–80° F | Rapid growing, highly decorative plant which can be used for group plantings or as a single plant. Very accommodating and recommended. |
| Hygrophila polysperma<br>Southeast Asia | high | 22–28° C<br>70–80° F | A beautiful species which is best appreciated as a group plant in all sizes of aquariums. |
| Limnophila species<br>Southeast Asia | high | 22–28° C<br>70–80° F | An especially beautiful and decorative group plant which should receive full light from above with the distance between the reflector and the plant being as short as possible. |
| Lobelia cardinalis<br>North America | high | 15–22° C<br>50–70° F | Requires full light. Given such, easily grows above the water surface. Should be planted in bunches. |
| Ludwigia species<br>All Warm Regions | high | 16–22° C<br>52–70° F | A highly accomodating, rapidly growing and recommended group plant. |
| Microsorium pteropus<br>Southeast Asia | moderate | 22–28° C<br>70–80103 F | An enduring fern which should not be planted but rather anchored to rocks and driftwood. |
| Myriophyllum species<br>Worldwide | high | 24° C<br>75° F | A rapid growing and extremely decorative group plant; not too high temperatures. |

| Scientific Name/Origin | Specifications | | |
|---|---|---|---|
| | Light | Temperature | Comments |
| Naja microdon<br>Tropical America | high | 20–28° C<br>68–80° F | A free-floating plant with many purposes. Will grow extremely rapidly. |
| Nomaphila stricta<br>Southeast Asia | high | 22–28° C<br>72–80° F | A decorative and enduring plant which should be planted in groups only in larger aquariums. Will benefit from frequent water changes. |
| Nuphar species<br>Southeast | high | 16–24° C<br>50–75° F | A very decorative single plant suitable for large aquariums only. |
| Riccia fluitans<br>Worldwide | high | 14–28° C<br>48–80° F | A free-floating easily culti-vated plant useful for spawn-ing fish. Benefits from fre-quent water changes. |
| Rotala macrandra<br>India | high to<br>very<br>high | 22–28° C<br>72–80° F | An extremely decorative group plant with rapid growth and very fine coloration of leaves. Benefits from a plant-ing the shortest distance pos-sible from reflector. |
| Rotala rotundifolia<br>Southeast Asia | high | 22–28° C<br>72–80° F | A group plant suitable for all sizes aquariums. Grows rapidly. |
| Sagittaria platyphylla<br>North America | high | 16–22° C<br>50–72° F | A highly recommended enduring plant suitable for many purposes but mainly as a background plant. |
| Samolus valerandi<br>America | very high | 14–20° C<br>48–68° F | A delicate foreground plant for coldwater aquariums only. Should be planted as short a distance from reflector as possible. |

| Scientific Name/Origin | Specifications | | |
|---|---|---|---|
| | **Light** | **Temperature** | **Comments** |
| Saururus cernuus<br>North America | high | 16–24° C<br>50–75° F | A highly decorative, easily cultivated plant which may be used alone as well as in a group. |
| Vallisneria gigantea<br>New Guinea, Philippines | high | 20–28° C<br>68–80° F | An easily cultivated plant which should be used only in the background. Suitable only for large, deep aquariums. |
| Vallisneria spiralis<br>Worldwide<br>Subtropical and<br>Tropical Regions | high | 16–24° C<br>50–75° F | A very enduring, highly recommended group plant. |
| Vesicularia dubyana<br>Indonesia, Philippines | high | 20–30° C<br>68–80° F | A very accommodated and delicate water moss which should be anchored to rocks or wood and not planted. Looks best in bunches in the foreground or middle of the aquarium. |

# AND FINALLY ...

## Snails and algae as pests

Two common pests in the aquarium are snails and algae.

*Snails* are by no means an essential part of any aquarium, and some species (particularly the "Malaysian livebearing snail") may develop to pest proportions. Try to avoid introducing snails to your aquarium, by rinsing all new plants in running water and avoiding the use of most live foods.

Snails can be controlled in a number of ways, including:

- introducing fish such as convict cichlids (*Cichlasoma nigrofasciatum*), clown loach (*Botia macracantha*), opaline gouramis (*Trichogaster trichopterus*) or puffer fish (*Tetraodon* sp.), all of which may feed on snails;
- placing one or two fish food tablets on an upturned saucer on the tank floor, and leaving it overnight. The snails will be attracted to the tablets, and can be removed with the saucer the next morning. This method will probably have to be repeated every night for a week or so, taking care to avoid letting uneaten tablets pollute the tank.
- chemical snail eradicators do exist, but these must be used *very* carefully, especially in a badly infested tank.

Even when present in large numbers, snails are usually unsightly rather than dangerous.

◁ *Two examples of beautiful sets of plants in an aquarium.*

If all else fails it may be necessary to completely strip the tank down, rinse all the rocks, gravel and decorations in dilute bleach or formalin (followed by a good rinse in water), and dip all the plants in a chemical snail eradicator or a dilute solution of potassium permanganate (again followed by a good rinse in water).

*Algae* can be a pest and many aquarists at some time experience problems with algae in their tanks. A heavy growth of algae over the inside of the tank (smothering rocks, plants, etc.) and excessively green water as a result of tiny suspended algal cells, are both signs that something is wrong with the routine maintenance of the aquarium. In order to control and subsequently prevent algal problems, several contributory factors need to be appreciated.

The relationship between the number of plants in the tank and the duration and intensity of the lighting is very important. Plants effectively control algae by absorbing available light energy, and nutrients from the water. In a well lit tank with too few plants, the light and nutrients will be used by the algae – which may thus develop into a problem. To control the algae, the lighting must be decreased, or the number of plants increased.

Every aquarist must be willing to vary the duration of lighting and number of plants to achieve a balance in his or her tank. For good plant growth, a shorter period of quite intense lighting is preferable to a longer period of more subdued lighting. In poorly lit tanks brown algae may become a problem.

Overfeeding aquarium fish causes a variety of problems, including the encouragement of algal growth. To avoid overfeeding it is essential to follow the "little and often" routine. Fish should be fed two to four times per day with only as much food as they can consume in a few minutes. Their digestive systems are better equipped to cope with frequent small meals.

It is important to realise that a little algae in a tank is quite beneficial and some fish enjoy feeding upon it. Excessive growths over the inside of the glass may be removed by a scraper, and siphoned out. Several remidies are available to control existing problems, and the regular use of *Spawning Aid* actually inhibits algal growth. Whenever advice is sought on the control of algae in aquaria it is important to realise the need to examine what factors within the tank brought about the algal problem to begin with. Chemical treatment is, of course, only the first step in its long term prevention and control.

*Malaysian livebearing snail*

*Red ramshorn snail, less of a pest*

*One method of controlling snails: a food tablet on a saucer*

*Flying Fox, Epalzeorhynchus siamensis, a useful algae eater*

# THE GOLDFISH AQUARIUM

## Natural habitat of the wild form: Eastern Asia

Does the goldfish have to swim around in circles in a little glass bowl? Do these creatures that bring life to our garden ponds with their darting activity have to spend the winter in a bath tub indoors? No! With a few pieces of bogwood and some well chosen decorative rocks a goldfish tank can be turned into an object of delight for children and adults alike. The goldfish has come a long way since it was a rather drab green/brown fish in its native China – some 1600 years ago. Selective breeding, originally by Eastern fish hobbyists (and later by Westerners) has now resulted in over 120 varieties – but all belonging to the same remarkable species – *Carassius auratus*.

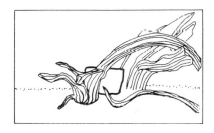

### Basic equipment

Minimum aquarium size 30 × 12 × 15 (tall) ins, contents about 12 gallons. 1–2 buckets of washed gravel, grain size ⅛ ins. Two large pieces of bogwood, one small piece, one large piece of coloured sandstone.

### The water

Temperature up to 25° C, although higher temperatures may be tolerated. Condition all new tapwater. No special requirements with regard to the water hardness or pH

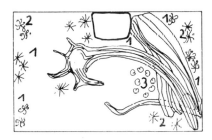

### Basic care

Change ⅓ water once a week. Any plants that are eaten must be replaced. Feed sparingly, twice a day. Check filters weekly.

### The fish

5 goldfish, *Carassius auratus* (**A**)
5 shubunkins (**B**)

### Why these fish?

Goldfish are wrongly regarded as merely a subject for beginners in the hobby. Nowadays there are so many different colour variants available that a nicely arranged and well lit goldfish aquarium is worthy of a special position in anyone's living room. Many goldfish are kept in the garden pond over the summer and will readily breed

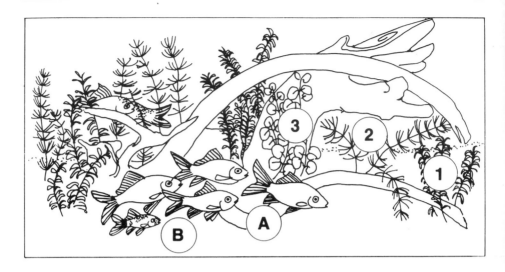

under such condition. Often fancy varieties will need to be over-wintered in a tub or some other container in a cellar or a garage though they could just as easily be used to enhance your lounge with their vivid colours and vivacious movements.

**The food**
Good quality flaked food; occasionally earthworms.

**The plants**
40 *Egeria densa* (**1**)

*A shubunkin, a beautiful hardy fish for the goldfish aqaurium. Photo: K. Paysan*

*Goldfish make lively, interesting aquarium fish.*          Photo: K. Paysan

20 stems of hornworth *Ceratophyllum demersum* (2)
5 creeping jenny *Lysimachia nummularia* (2)

### Why these plants?

Goldfish are great plant eaters and for this reason you should only have fast growing, robust plants in your aquarium. They will also be useful generators of oxygen. The hornwort in particular is likely to be consumed avidly and therefore needs to be replaced rather frequently. However, it is easy to grow your own replacement stock in a bucket outdoors if you cannot obtain enough from your dealer. Even those shoots that have been severely nibbled will re-shoot once left alone. In fact, creeping jenny is not a true aquatic plant though it will survive for a long time in the aquarium and often thrive over a period of many years, putting out lots of fresh shoots. It is hardy and is not eaten by the goldfish.

### Additional equipment

Polyfoam filter or an efficient power filter. Spray bar for additional aeration in warm weather. Leave filter(s) running continuously. Lighting from two fluorescent tubes, each 20 watts. Thermometer to check water temperature.

# FANCY GOLDFISH

## Natural habitat of the wild form: Eastern Asia

Like the more familiar common goldfish and shubunkin (see previous pages), these exotic or "fancy" goldfish varieties have been produced by careful patient selective breeding by Man.

Actually, fancy goldfish like veiltails can be kept in the same way as they were in their original Far Eastern home. There they were kept in large shallow containers and observed from above. In this way the graceful flowing movements of their long fins could be fully appreciated. A set-up aquarium also appeals for the same reason.

### Basic equipment
Large aquarium measuring at least 48 × 18 × 18 (tall) ins and containing at least 50 gallons. Washed gravel with grain size up to ⅓ ins.

### The water
Many people keep fancy goldfish at room temperature, although experience shows that they will do well (and even thrive) at 30° C and above. All new water must be conditioned with a conditioner; no special requirements with regard to water hardness and pH.

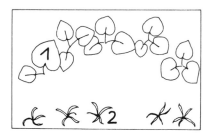

### Basic care
Change at least ⅓ of the water every week. Powerful filtration is needed as large goldfish have correspondingly large appetites (especially at warm temperatures) – and produce large amounts of waste material. Plants will have to be replaced quite frequently. Add plant fertilisier at every water change. Feet 2 or 3 times a day, but sparingly.

### The food
Good quality dried foods, some "safe" live foods.

### The fish
Fancy gold fish (*Carassius auratus*) such as veiltail (A), telescoped-eyed veiltail (B), red cap oranda (C). Tank to accommodate up to 20 medium to large fancy goldfish.

*The long, flowing fins of some fancy goldfish, like this red-cap oranda, can become ragged and inflamed if kept in water that is too cool.*                    *Photo: K. Paysan*

### Why these fish?

Fancy goldfish, especially large and therefore expensive ones, need a large and well cared for aquarium if they are to thrive. They are not as hardy as the common goldfish, but the extra care they require is worth it, as anyone who has kept a tank full of these magnificent fish will agree.

### The plants

Yellow water lilies (*Nupher luteum*) **(1)**.
Giant arrow head (*Sagittaria latifolia*) **(2)**

### Why these plants?

Many fancy goldfish (in fact, goldfish in general) have a mixed diet which can include vegetable matter. Therefore, the plants must be selected so that they are either too tough to be eaten, or else appear unpalatable to the fish. Goldfish do not seem to like the taste of water lily leaves, and *Sagittaria* is usually a little too tough for them. In fact the plants also seem to lend an oriental flavour to the tank.

### Additional equipment

An efficient power filter plus spray bar and (perhaps) a heater-thermostat. Lighting from 2–4 40 watt fluorescent tubes or 1–2 125 watt metal halide or mercury vapour lamps. Thermometer to check tank temperature.

*The black moor is a strikingly unusual fish for a large indoor aquarium.*

*Photo: K. Paysan*

# LIVEBEARING TOOTHCARPS

## Natural habitat of the wild forms: South America

This whole tank is dominated by the decorative shape of the heart-leafed Amazonian sword plant, *Echinodorus cordifolius*. Even *Echinodorus bleheri* – which in itself could well constitute a fine specimen plant in the tank – is used here as a mere background plant. The plants are chosen to give a wide range of green shades, to do full justice to the array of colours displayed by the tank bred forms of livebearing toothcarps, some of the most lively aquarium fish.

### Basic equipment
Minimum aquarium size 30 × 12 × 15 (tall) ins, contents about 12 gallons. Four large greenish-grey pieces of rock, about one bucket of washed gravel, grain size ⅛ ins, and on top this about ½ inch of coarse river gravel of different shades.

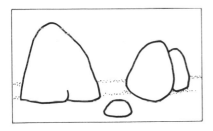

### The water
Temperature range 24–26° C. Tapwater should be conditioned before use and the pH value around neutral. No special requirements in terms of water hardness – it can be very hard.

### Basic care
Change ⅓ of the water every 3–4 weeks. The plants that were originally set out soon grow quickly and need to be thinned. Always condition all new water, and use suitable plant fertilisers too.

### The fish
Sixteen fermale, eight male guppies (*Poecilia reticulata*) (**A**)
Two pairs platies (*Xiphophorus maculatus*)
Two pairs blue platies (*Xiphophorus maculatus*) (**B**)
Two pairs coral platies (*Xiphophorus maculatus*) (**C**)
Two pairs wagtail platies (*Xiphophorus maculatus*) (**D**)
Two pairs lyretail black mollies (*Poecilia sphenops*) (**E**)

### Why these fish?
An aquarium filled with this type of lively colourful fish can be a beautiful sight. The guppies with their large colourful tail dominate the tank. Each guppy can be differ-

ently marked and each of their tails has a different colour pattern. Even the females are no longer as monotonous as the females of the wild form and have large colourful tails. In order to bring a couple of centres of calm into this lively community, various platies are also included and the strike the observer with the difference in their behaviour and colouring. The matt black shades of the lyretail black mollies are also very effective, and they also act as excellent algae control agents.

**The food**
Good quality flaked foods.

**The plants**
8 Amazonian sword plants
(*Echinodorus bleheri*) **(1)**

*A delicately marked male guppy
Photo: K. Paysan*

*Nowadays male guppies are available with a wide range of fin shapes and colour-ation, but they can all freely interbreed with other females.   Photos: K. Knaack*

2 Amazonian sword plant
(*Echinodorus cordifolius*) **(2)**
1 Amazonian sword plants
(*Echinodorus aschersonianus*) **(3)**
3 broad leaved arrowwort (*Sagittaria platy-phylla*) **(4)**
20 dwarf arrowwort (*Sagittaria subulata f. pusilla*) **(5)**

**Why these plants?**
The broad leaves of *Echinodorus bleheri* cover the background and give the impression of an aquarium that recedes into a deep jungle of plants. The heart shaped leaves of *Echinodorus cordifolius* help make it the dominant plant in the aqurium. Its leaves make a magnificent backdrop and contrast to the activity of the colourful guppies. The dwarf arrowwort liven up the floor of the tank and will soon cover it entirely.

**Additional equipment**
Filtration from a polyfoam filter, or a small power filter. Leave running all the time and maintain regularly.   Heater-thermostat, and thermometer. Lighting from 2 fluorescent tubes, 20 watt each.

101

# HARD WATER COMMUNITY TANK

## Suitable fish from around the world

Large pieces of limestone, riddled with holes, will provide a suitable environment and plenty of hideaways for a multitude of fish species originating from hard waters all around the world. In this instance, the emphasis in the layout is an arrangement of rocks because most of the fish are plant-eaters and the majority of aquarium plants will not tolerate very hard water.

### Basic equipment
Minimum aquarium size 30 × 12 × 15 (tal) ins, contents about 20 gallons. About two buckets of washed gravel, grain size ⅛ ins, one bucket of fine river sand, 7 large pieces of limestone (with holes).

### The water
Temperature range 24–28° C; hardness more than 20° general hardness; condition tapwater before use; pH value neutral to slightly alkaline.

### Basic care
Change ⅓ water once a week, adding a suitable tapwater conditioner.

### The fish
Five pairs dwarf rainbow fish (*Melanotaenia macculochi*) (**A**)
Two pairs rainbow fish (*Melanotaenia nigrans*) (**B**)
Two pairs rainbow fish (*Melanotaenia affinis*) (**C**)
Two archer fish (*Toxotes jaculator*) (**D**)
One pair *Pseudotropheus* sp. (**E**)
Two pairs *Labidochromis caeruleus likomae* (**F**)
One spotted catfish (*Plecostomus punctatus*)

### Why these fish?
Sometimes it is difficult to keep more than one pair of fully grown Malawi cichlids together because of their pugnacious temperament. For this reason the fish for this aquarium were selected on the basis of compatibility of their colouring and temperament, and although the may be inclined to chase each other, at least they do not bite lumps out of their companions! The *Pseudotropheus* will keep mostly to the lower

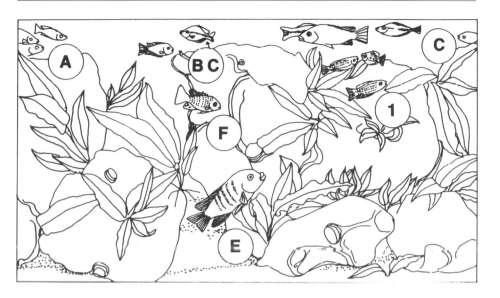

regions of the tank whilst the shoals of rainbow fish swim about in the free swimming areas in the upper tank – and the archer fish are a purely surface fish.

**The food**

Good quality flaked and freeze-dried foods.

*A close-up of the spitting mouthparts of the archer fish.*     Photo: G. Ott

*A beautiful suckermouth catfish,* Plecostomus, *which will thrive in quite hard water.*
Photo: L. Wischnath

## The plants
15 Java ferns (*Microsorium pteropus*) **(1)**

### Why these plants?
The large leaves of the Java fern provide an effective contrast to the light coloured rocks. Its coarse leaves are not eaten by the fish and its fine, threadlike clumps of roots afford ready hiding places for any fish that are being pursued. Whereas many aquatic plants do not thrive in such hard water, the Java fern grows very well. In addition, common hornwort (*Ceratophyllum*) can be kept which – although it is often eaten – is a fast grower and produces plenty of oxygen.

### Additional equipment
Efficient power filter with spray bar. Lighting from 2 fluorescent tubes, each 20 watts. Regular checks using test kits to measure pH and water hardness. Heater-thermostat, thermometer.

*A arches fish,*
Toxotes jaculater

# Soft Water Community Tank

## Suitable fish from around the world

A single, large specimen plant dominates the centre of this aquarium with a number of dense clumps of plants scattered around the sides and rear of the tank. A barrier of rocks divides the foreground and background into distinct areas. Shoals of small fish swim back and forth with swordtails acting as colour highlights amongst them.

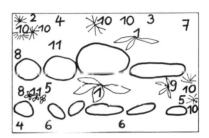

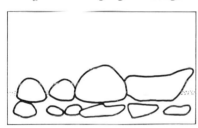

### Basic equipment

Minimum aquarium size 30 × 12 × 15 (tall) ins, contents about 20 gallons. Two or three buckets of washed gravel which should be calcium free, with grain size around ⅛ ins. Three large rocks are used to screen off the rear and 5 medium sized stones provide a gradual descent to the foreground. Ten smoothly rounded stones are scattered at irregular intervals on the bed. Avoid calcium bearing rocks and stones, as well as gravel.

### The water

Temperature range 24–26° C, hardness up to 10° general hardness, pH slightly acid. Excessively hard water must be softened; use a blackwater "tonic" too.

### Basic care

Because of the high population housed in the tank powerful filtration is required. The fast growing plants will need to be regularly thinned or pruned; remove any decaying leaves. A one third water change will be needed every 2 weeks, adding water conditioners and plant fertilisers. Top up with soft water, replacing any evaporated water with previously softened water.

### The fish

Three pairs Rasbora boraplensis (**A**)
15 Harlequins (*Rasbora hengeli*) (**B**)
5 Harlequins (*Rasbora heteromorpha*) (**C**)
Five pairs Three-line rasbora (*Rasbora trilineata*) (**D**)
Two pairs Sparkling panchax (*Aplocheilus lineatus*) (**E**)
10 Serpae tetra (*Hyphessobrycon callistus*) (**F**)
Two pairs Swordtails (*Xiphophorus helleri*) (**G**)
2 *Otocinclus affinis*
1 *Ancistrus cirrhosus*
2 *Loricaria filamentosa*

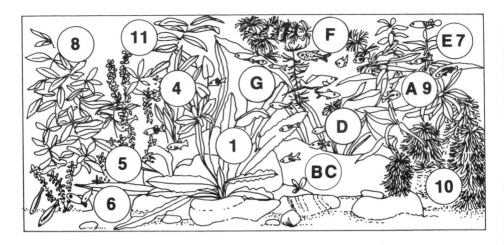

## Why these fish?

Someone who just wants to have a tank full of beautiful fish in the lounge should not always base their purchases on geographical considerations, but rather put together a selection of species according to their personal taste. Here we show such a tank, containing a wealth of colours, shapes and vitality. All the zones of the aquarium are occupied; the bed by the catfish, the surface by the harlequin fish, with the shoals of other fish swimming between the two.

## The food

Good quality flaked and freeze-dried foods.

*Two* Loricaria filamentosa *catfish.*          *Photo: W. Armbrust*

Rasbora daniconius *should be more freely available in the trade.*        *Photo: B. Kahl*

## The plants
2 giant Amazon sword plants (*Echinodorus maior*) **(1)**
3 *Cryptocoryne balansae* **(2)**
3 *Cryptocoryne ciliata* **(3)**
3 *Cryptocoryne cordate* **(4)**
3 *Cryptocoryne affinis* **(5)**
10 dwarf cryptocorynes (*Cryptocoryne willisii*) **(6)**
1 *Hygrophila difformis* **(7)**
20 Indian water star (*Hygrophila polysperma*) **(8)**
2 *Hygrophila polysperma* – brownish form **(9)**
15 *Limnophila sessiflora "ambulia"* **(10)**
20 *Rotalia rotundifolia* **(11)**

## Why these plants?
We have here a community of plants from all over the world and a number of cryptocorynes that might well be worthy of a place of honour, remain tucked away in the background here. With the large specimen plants in the middle, there is still sufficient swimming room because the others are planted along the edges of the tank.

## Additional equipment
Power filter, using peat as one of the media. Lighting from 2 fluorescent tubes, each 20 watts. Possibly an ion exchanger for preparing soft water, and a $CO_2$ diffuser to encourage plants. Test kits to measure pH and hardness. Heater-thermostat, thermometer.

# Fish from South-East Asia

## Fish from a tropical Asian river

The clear water of a slow flowing river has dense, rapid growing plants in the zones near its banks. Barbs and danios play in the shallows, while the deeper parts are inhabited by fish like *Pristolepis* and loach.

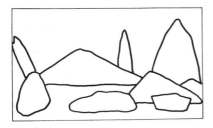

### Basic equipment

Minimum aquarium size 30 × 12 × 15 (tall) ins, contents about 12 gallons. 1–2 buckets of washed gravel, grain size ⅛ ins. 10 pieces of shiny slate about hand size are placed in such a way as to form small cavities close to the gravel bed. By planting little circles of plants various separate free swimming areas are created.

### The water

Temperature range 24–26° C; treat tapwater with a good quality conditioner. No special requirements in terms of water hardness.

### Basic care

Every three weeks change ⅓ of the water, adding suitable plant fertilisers afterwards. Regular thinning and pruning of the *Rotala* and Indian water stars is required. Collect up any dying leaves.

### The fish

Four pairs Sumatra barbs (*Barbus tetrazona*) **(A)**
Four pairs cherry barbs (*Barbus titteya*)
Five pairs zebra danios (*Brachydanio rerio*) **(B)**
Five pairs pearl danios (*Brachydanio albolineatus*) **(C)**
Four pairs giant danios (*Danio malabaricus*) **(D)**
1 *Pristolepis fasciata*
4 loach (*Acanthophthalmus semicinctus*)
*South American fish as algae eaters:*
1 *Ancistrus* species
2 *Otocinclus affinis*

### Why these fish?

The fish were selected in the light of the fact that most of them come from the same continent. They are intended to liven up all the water zones. For instance, the Sumatra barb swims in all areas. The cherry barb likes to hang around in largish shoals in the

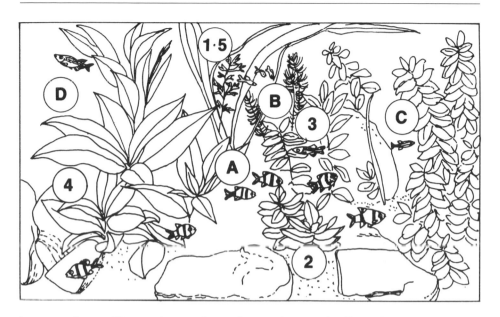

lower regions. Giant zebra and pearl danios are usually found around the surface. *Pristolepis fasciata* is a placid denizen of the area close to the bed and the loach are bottom dwellers. *Ancistrus* will graze algae from the rocks and glass while the catfish can be relied on to keep the leaves free of algae.

*An ever active shoal of zebra danios.*              *Photo: K. Paysan*

*The Sumatran or tiger barb is available in a number of tank-bred forms. Photo: K. Paysan*

## The food
Good quality flaked and freeze-dried foods.

## The plants
3 *Crinum thaianum* **(1)**
20 *Rotala macranda* **(2)**
20 fine-leafed rotala (*Rotala wallichii*) **(3)**
20 round-leafed rotala (*Rotala rotundifolia*)
6 giant *Hygrophila corymbosa* **(4)**
3 Indian water star (*Hygrophila difformis*) **(5)**

## Why these plants?
The *Crinum thaianum* with their long, strap like leaves stand against the fast growing *Rotala* and Indian water stars. The giant *Hygrophila* acts as a contrast to the *Rotala macranda*: light green and large leafed against red and small leafed. *Rotala wallichii* and *Rotala macranda* are eaten by the barbs but the plants will soon make up for any losses if well cared for.

## Additional equipment
Power filter, with aeration from spray bar. Lighting from 2 fluorescent tubes, each 20 watts. Heater-thermostat, thermometer.

# A TANK FOR MBUNA CICHLIDS

## Natural habitat: Lake Malawi, Africa

A colourful group of these fish is always an interesting, lively sight. You may have one male spreading his gills in a display gesture, while his weaker rival retreats to the safety of a crack in the rocks. One might be tempted to think that this kind of reaction was brought about by the weight of numbers present in the tank and the behaviour might be seen as somewhat untypical or unnatural. But this is not the case; in Lake Malawi the population density in many places is just as high.

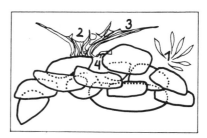

Two pairs zebra cichlids *Pseudotropheus zebra* (B)
Four pairs zebra cichlids *Pseudotropheus spec. affin. zebra* (C)
Four pairs red zebras *Pseudotropheus spec. affin. zebra* (D)
Two pairs *Melanochromis johannii* (E)
Four pairs parrot snouted cichlids *Labeotropheus trewavasae* (F)
6 *Haplochromis moorii* (G)

### Why these fish?
In a display tank of this kind one really has to show as many different species from Lake Malawi as possible. Those that are being kept in this tank are all about the same size and equally powerful. They will settle down well with one another, and any disputes will be resolved with mere threats rather than actual fights. Pairs frequently spawn and since they are mouthbrooders their fry may actually survive and grow well.

### Basic equipment
A large display tank contents about 200 gallons. Gravel with a grain size of ⅛ ins. 25 large coloured sandstone slabs, glued together with aquarium scaler in such a way that they form a large number of unconnected fissures and cavities. This rocky fortress is constructed in the middle of the tank so that the free swimming room is above at the front, the sides and at the top of the tank.

### The water
The temperature range 24–26° C; treat tapwater with a conditioner. pH value neutral to slightly alkaline. It can be very hard.

### The fish
Four pairs *Pseudotropheus socolofi* (A)

### Basic care
More than ⅓ of the water is changed every week. Decaying matter and faeces is carefully removed with a siphon tube.

### The food
Good quality flaked and freeze-dried foods.

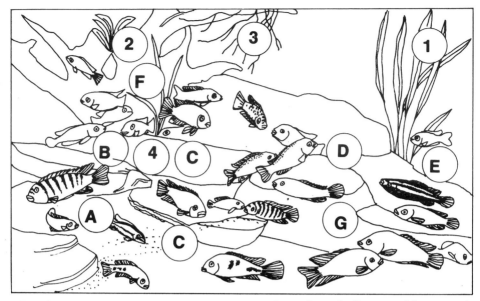

## The plants

5 *Cryptocoryne balansae* (1)
5 Java ferns *Microsorium pteropus* (2)
The dangling roots of a philodendron (3)
5 giant eel grass *Vallisneria gigantea* (4)

### Why these plants?

Of all the plants put into this aquarium only the *Cryptocoryne balansae* lasted the course. All the others had to be replaced fairly often. The very leafy philodendron that grows over the tank takes a lot of the products of metabolism out of the water via its roots.

### Additional equiment

A power filter with spray bar for aeration. Lighting from 5 fluorescent tubes, 40–65 watts each or mercury vapour or 2–3 metal halide lights, 125 watts each. Testkits to measure water hardness, pH, and perhaps ammonia. Heater-thermostat, thermometer.

Pseudotropheus *zebra is available in a number of colour forms, whose taxonomic status may be uncertain.* Photos: *R. Zieschang*

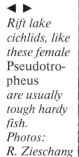

◄ ►
*Rift lake cichlids, like these female* Pseudotropheus *are usually tough hardy fish.* Photos: *R. Zieschang*

# A TROPICAL SOUTH AMERICAN TANK

## Natural habitat: Amazonian stream

An aquascape designed to re-create the bank region of a river in the South American jungle. Characins, cichlids and catfish live here.

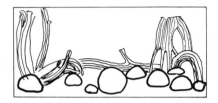

### Basic equipment

Minimum aquarium size 36 × 12 × 12 ins, contents about 15 gallons. Two or three buckets of washed gravel, grain size ⅛ ins. 10 rounded river boulders in granite or red sandstone and about 20 other rounded river pebbles and 5 large bogwood roots make up the rest of the decoration.

### The water

Temperature range 24–26° C, hardness up to 10° general hardness, condition tapwater and add a blackwater tonic, pH value slightly acid to neutral.

### Basic care

Change ⅓ water every three weeks and add plant fertilisers. The common hornwort is a rampant grower and needs to be thinned at frequent intervals. Any dying leaves should be removed. Debris should be removed using a siphon tube.

### The food

Good quality flaked and freeze-dried foods.

### The fish

One pair angelfish (*Pterophyllum scalare*, hybrid form) (**A**)
One pair wild caught angelfish (*Pterophyllum scalare*) (**B**)
Four pairs Ramirez's dwarf cichlid (*Papiliochromis ramirezi*) (**C**)
Trio *Moenkhausia pittieri* (**D**)
Trio *Hyphessobrycon ornatus* (**E**)
Two pairs *Megalomphodus megalopterus* (**F**)
Three pairs *Megalomphodus sweglesi* (**G**)
Three pairs lemon tetras (*Hyphessobrycon pulchripinnis*) (**H**)
Trio pretty tetras (*Hemmigrammus pulcher*) (**I**)
15 golden tetras (*Hemmigrammus armstrongi*) (**K**)
10 neon tetras (*Paracheirodon innesi*) (**L**)
1 *Ancistrus cirrhosus*
2 *Otocinclus affinis*
5 armoured catfish (*Corydoras myersi*)

### Why these fish?

Practically all these fish are placid, peaceful subjects that respect each other's territories. The beautiful, highly coloured little tetras with their pretty fins make a nice contrast to the larger angelfish. The specimen of *Ancistrus* will graze on all the algae on the bogwood, rocks and panes and the *Otocinclus* will clear up any that grows on the leaves. The armoured catfish fit in well with the colours of the tetras and contrast nicely with the shape of the angelfish. The species selected here ensures that all levels of the water are full of life. A particularly

conspicuous inhabitant of the tank bottom are the *Papiliochromis ramirezi* – with their interesting courtship and breeding behaviour.

## The plants

2 broad-leaved Amazonian sword plants (*Echinodorus bleheri*) **(1)**

2 giant Amazonian sword plants (*Echinodorus maior*) **(2)**

1 *Echinodorus parviflorus* **(3)**

2 patches of grassy plants, each consisting of about 200 specimens (*Lilaeopis noveazelandia*) **(4)**

1 patch slender spike rush (*Eleocharis aciularis*) **(5)**

10 shoots of common hornwort (*Ceratophyllum demersum*) **(6)**

## Why these plants?

In the course of time the brod leaved Amazonian sword plants will grow into bushy

*Ramirez's dwarf cichlid is beautiful but a little delicate.*     Photos: H. Linke

125

*Red phantom tetras,* Megalamphodus sweglesi.          *Photo: K. Paysan*

clumps, providing a beautiful touch to the one side. The giant Amazonian sword plant, with its runners and light leaves, makes a splendid specimen plant and forms a nice contrast to the dark hues of the *Echinodorus parviflorus.* The clumps of the various grass like plants also help to constitute little territories, though without encroaching on the free swimming room of the angelfish. The common hornwort makes a fine backdrop to the whole, often glimmering with a greeny gold hue. The

fast growing plants use up many of the products of the fishes' metabolic processes and produce a great deal of oxygen if given plenty of light.

## Additional equipment

A power filter, perhaps with additional aeration from a spray bar. Lighting from 3 fluorescent tubes, each 30 watts, or better still 125 watt mercury vapour lamp. Test kits to monitor pH and water hardness. Heater-thermostat, thermometer.

# A WEST AFRICAN TANK

## Natural habitat: tropical West Africa

This re-creates the bankside of a West African river, with marsh plants growing amongst purely aquatic plants. The gaps between the stones provide hiding places for cichlids. Shoals of small barbs and characins dart around, looking for food.

### Basic equipment

Minimum aquarium size 30 × 12 × 15 (tall) ins, contents about 12 gallons. 1–2 buckets washed gravel, grain size ⅛ ins. 9 flat stones of lime-free rock are carefully placed in layers so as to form a series of caves that are not connected with each other. The cichlids will dig up the bed of the tank and so the rocks should be glued together with aquarium sealer.

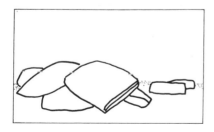

### The water

Temperature range 24–26° C, hardness up to 10° general hardness. Treat tapwater with a conditioner adding a blackwater tonic. pH slightly acid to neutral. Hard water has to be softened.

### Basic care

Change ⅓ of the water every three weeks, adding conditioner and plant fertilisers. The *Najas* plants will need to be thinned out in order to prevent the free swimming area from becoming clogged up. Remove any dead or decaying leaves.

### The food

Good quality flaked and freeze-dried foods.

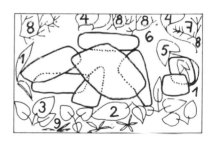

### The fish

10 Congo tetra (*Micralestes interruptus*) (**A**)
15 *Barbus bariloides* (**B**)
One pair *Pelvicachromis pulcher* (**B**)
Three pairs *Nanochromis nudiceps* (**C**)
Trio of *Epiplatys fasciolatus* (**D**)
Two Butterfly fish (*Pantodon buchholzi*)
Two pairs Thomas' dwarf cichlid (*Pelmatochromis thomasi*) (**E**)
Algae eaters from South America
1 *Ancistrus* species
2 *Otocinclus affinis*

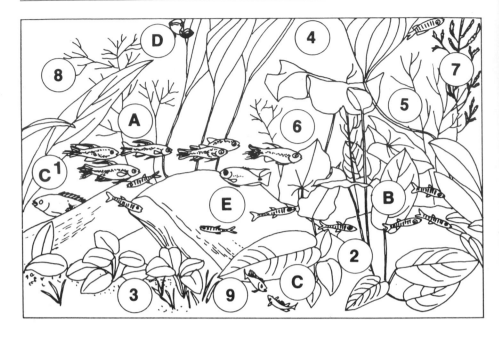

## Why these fish?

The *Epiplatys* and butterfly fish are surface fish, *Micralestes* and the barbs are for the middle water regions, and the cichlids are bottom and cave dwelling subjects, to ensure that all the water levels are occupied. The red and yellow shades of the *Pelvicachromis pulcher* go well with the blue of the *Nannochromis* and the sheen of the Congo tetras (*Micralestes*).

*Pelvicachromis pulcher is another cichlid that exists in a number of forms, as these males clearly show. (see also page 130 below)* Photos: H. Linke

*The Congo tetra,* Micralestes interruptus. Photo: K. Paysan

## The plants

4 West African *Anubias lanceolata* **(1)**
2 *Anubias barteri* **(2)**
10 *Anubias nana* (dwarf species) **(3)**
3 *Ottelia alismoides* **(4)**
1 red *Nymphaea lotus* **(5)**
1 green *Nymphaea lotus* **(6)**
5 *Bolbitis heudelotii* **(7)**
50 *Najas* sp. **(8)**
20 African eel grass (*Vallisneria* sp.) **(9)**

## Why these plants?

One frequently finds various species of *Anubias* growing immersed on the banks of streams and rivers in West Africa. The plants are regularly flooded in the rainy season but continue to grow. This is why they lend themselves readily to aquarium cultivation. Their hard leaves can withstand the attentions of any fish that eat vegetation. *Ottelia* is a large, annual plant that sends a rapid succession of funnel like leaves up to the surface. The *Najas* is a rampant grower and helps take care of the biological cleansing of the water.

## Additional equipment

A power filter or poly-foam filter and heater-thermostat plus thermometer. Lighting from 2 fluorescent tubes each 20 watts. Test kits to measure pH and hardness.